Religion

and

the

Public

Square

in

the

21st

Century

RELIGION AND THE PUBLIC SQUARE
IN THE 21ST CENTURY

Proceedings from the conference
The Future of Government Partnerships with the Faith Community
April 25-26, 2000

at Wingspread
Racine, Wisconsin

sponsored by
The Welfare Policy Center
of Hudson Institute
and
The Johnson Foundation

Edited by
Ryan Streeter

with a Preface by
John J. DiIulio, Jr.

Contributors:
*Stanley Carlson-Thies, Dan Coats, E. J. Dionne, Don Eberly,
Carl Esbeck, Amy Sherman, and Ryan Streeter*

Religion and the Public Square in the 21st Century
Proceedings from the conference:
The Future of Government Partnerships with the Faith Community
Edited by Ryan Streeter
ISBN 1-55813-127-2
$11.95

Copyright © 2001 Hudson Institute, Inc.
Herman Kahn Center
5395 Emerson Way
Indianapolis, IN 46226, U.S.A.
For speaking engagements and/or media interviews, contact Hudson Institute: 317-545-1000
Orders only: 888-554-1325
www.hudson.org

Printed in the United States of America.

CONTENTS

During presidential campaign 2000, both Texas Governor George W. Bush and Vice President Al Gore made speeches calling for greater government/religious partnerships to address urban and social problems. Each candidate also spoke openly and often about his own faith commitments as a born-again Christian. Gore's running mate, Senator Joseph Lieberman, an orthodox Jew, was so full of "God talk" that the Anti-Defamation League of B'nai Brith gave him a public scolding. The senator replied politely but firmly that he would keep his faith on public display.

If certain leading observers are right, then our pious presidential politicians (excepting Defense Secretary Dick Cheney, who remained mum on the Almighty) simply are reflecting recent social trends that favor spiritual "identity politics." Nobel-prize winning economist Robert Fogel professes that America is in the early stages of a Fourth Great Awakening. Reverend Jim Wallis, who directs a national umbrella organization of churches concerned about poverty and racism, quips that the country has gone from asking whether "God is dead" to debating whether "angels are real." Likewise, George Gallup, Jr., the eminent pollster, avers that, despite declines in church attendance, Americans remain a super-religious people. Indeed, Gallup reports that more Americans than ever are moderately to intensely "spiritual" in their everyday lives and self-understandings, and that many traditional or orthodox religious orientations are gaining, not losing, adherents.

I seriously doubt that America is experiencing religious revival. Fresh converts to web-site pornography and psychic phone lines probably outnumber new seekers after old-time religion (double-counting aside). Still, it seems plain to me that political discourse, and, in turn, public laws and policies at all levels and across all branches of government, are, for whatever reasons, becoming more "faith friendly."

This de-secularizing secular trend in favor of religion in the public square is incremental but unmistakable. For instance, since the mid-1980s, federal and state courts alike have been chipping away at super-strict separation of church and state doctrines. Charitable Choice, section 104 of the federal government's 1996 welfare law, encourages states to use faith-based organizations in serving the poor and needy, and requires that religious organizations be permitted to receive contracts, vouchers, and other government funding on virtually the same basis as any other nongovernmental providers of services. Importantly, Charitable Choice explicitly protects the religious character of faith-based organizations that are willing to accept public funds.

True, the number of faith-based organizations receiving federal dollars today via Charitable Choice remains paltry (only one, for example, in Philadelphia, a city with over 2,000 churches, synagogues, mosques, and other community-serving congregations), but the provision is momentous nonetheless. A prediction: as faith-friendly coalitions within Congress get on the same page of the social policy hymnal with a pro-religion president, and despite dissents from each party's base (secular libertarians among Republicans, secular liberals among Democrats), Charitable Choice will be retained, implemented, and expanded to other areas of federal social policy before 2004.

Already, the new faith-friendly spirit of the public laws has wrought some government/religious partnerships that give even many faith-friendly partisans pause. For example, several years ago the Texas Department of Criminal Justice gave an entire prison over to ex-Watergate felon Charles W. Colson's Prison Fellowship, an expressly evangelical Christian organization dedicated spiritually to religious conversion and empirically to the proposition that accepting Jesus Christ as Lord and Savior is the "only" cure for youth crime, prisoner recidivism, and violence. (Yes, George W. Bush was very much behind the contract, and, judging by frequency of public references, Prison Fellowship is easily his single favorite example of faith in action.)

Few public agencies have gone that far, but, all across the country, state and local policymakers, both liberal and conservative, both Democratic and Republican, have begun experimenting, or searching for ways to experiment, with problem-focused public/private partnerships involving hitherto unprecedented collaboration between governments and religious organizations. To cite just one characteristic example, in Philadelphia, Democratic mayor John Street has directed each city public school to "adopt," or be adopted by, a nearby church for the purpose of developing joint after-school, literacy training, and other programs.

What is wonderful about the proceedings of the Wingspread conference contained herein is that they reflect a robust diversity of informed views about the present extent, potential efficacy, practical scalability, and constitutional propriety of government partnerships with faith communities. In a recent Brookings Institution edited volume, one Wingspread participant, *Washington Post* syndicated columnist E. J. Dionne, and I tried to represent competing legal, theological, empirical, and political perspectives on religion in the public square.[1] I think we did a pretty good job, but the Wingspread papers refine and enlarge our understanding of the subject in ways that should make the Hudson Institute and the Johnson Foundation, co-sponsors of the conference, quite proud.

Like myself, each contributor to these proceedings harbors various doubts about religion in the public square. In the end, however, each contributor resolves these doubts in a manner that renders him or her largely at one with the day's faith-friendly political and policy currents. Let me preface these proceedings, therefore, by briefly weighing in with parting questions informed by my nearly six years of professional study and personal activism on the subject, and grounded in my three interlocking chauvinisms toward it: Catholic, scientific, and pluralistic.

Catholic

In the letter that begins the latest English edition of the *Catechism of the Catholic Church*, Pope John Paul II reminds us: "If faith is not expressed in works, it is dead (cf. *Jas* 2:14-16) and cannot bear fruit unto eternal life."[2] My Catholic bible translates the relevant verses from James as follows:

> What good is it, my brothers, if someone says he has faith but does not have works? Can that faith save him? If a brother or a sister has nothing to wear and has no food for the day, and one of you says to them, "Go in peace, keep warm, and eat well," but you do not give them the necessities of the body, what good is it? So also faith of itself, if it does not have works, is dead.

The Church's canonical embrace of "faith without works is dead" is evident throughout the *Catechism*, but most especially in its sections on "Social Justice" and its explication of the Seventh Commandment's prohibition against stealing:

> How can we not recognize Lazarus, the hungry beggar in the parable (cf. *Lk* 17:19-31), in the multitude of human beings without bread, a roof or a place to stay? How can we fail to hear Jesus: "As you did it not to one of the least of these, you did it not to me" (Mt 25:45)?

Many evangelical Christians still preach fire and brimstone against the Church and *Jas* 2:14-16, arguing, for example, that "faith without works is dead" teaching flatly contradicts Paul's teaching (see especially *Rom* 4: 5-6). Actually, Paul argues against those who claim salvation based solely on *either* works alone *or* faith alone. Elsewhere, Paul teaches that "faith working through love" naturally begets a life of self-sacrifice in which true believers "bear one another's burdens" to "fulfill the law of Christ" (see especially *Gal* 5, 6).

But various evangelical Christian churches and organizations are self-consciously warming to works. In developing community-serving ministries to the poor, the homeless, the imprisoned, and others among "the least of these," ever more Protestants—urban and suburban; black, white, and Latino; local and national—are "reinventing" Catholic social teaching. Several recent books by evangelical leaders (Charles W. Colson and Ronald J. Sider come immediately to mind) strongly echo Catholic social teaching, and I have even heard Pentecostals explicitly preach James.

There are, however, aspects of the Catholic community-serving ministry experience that both Protestants and other faith communities ought to avoid. For example, organizations like Catholic Charities embody too much works, not enough faith. In much (though by no means all) of what it does and how it does it, Catholic Charities, which receives about two-thirds of its budget from government, is virtually indistinguishable from a secular social welfare agency. Somewhere between the strictly secularized, all-works components of a Catholic Charities and the no-James, conversion-only, faith-alone tradition is, or so I believe, the brightest possible future of government partnerships with faith communities.

Scientific

Based on careful, detailed field surveys by my Penn colleague Ram A. Cnaan and others, we know for sure that, throughout urban America, faith-based organizations serve their needy neighbors. For example, Philadelphia's community-serving churches, synagogues, and mosques supply a conservatively estimated quarter-billion dollars a year worth of social services to the city's poorest children, youth, and families.[3] The primary beneficiaries of the congregations' good works are poor neighborhood children who are not members (and whose families are not members) of the congregations that serve them. Catholic schools that serve non-Catholic, low-income African-American populations, and small- and medium-sized black churches themselves, are in the community-serving ministry vanguard.[4]

Granted, the faith communities are out there doing much social and civic good according to their own lights and from within their own organizations. But is there conclusive evidence that they can collaborate across the usual racial and denominational lines and work in public/private, religious/secular, urban/suburban partnerships? Can the massive volunteer base represented by these religious organizations be systematically mobilized into programs that, for example, make church-based after-school literacy training available to public school children citywide, or that make caring, responsible adult mentors available to the country's over two million children of incarcerated parents? The Cnaan data and lots of inspiring anecdotes suggest that the answers may well justify the growing faith in faith-based approaches. In Philadelphia and other cities, I am at work on various research and program development projects that may take us beyond what we already know on this policy-relevant score, which to date is not very much; stay tuned.

There is a good and growing body of empirical evidence, compiled by my Penn colleague Byron Johnson and others, which indicates that, other things being equal, religious commitment reduces crime, delinquency, and other forms of socioeconomic failure and deviance. For example, studies show that young black urban males who attend church regularly are less likely to succumb to the blandishments of drugs and crime than otherwise comparable but "unchurched" black youth.[5]

But there are yet many contrary findings that call into question the "resiliency" benefits of church attendance and other attachments to religion; and, even if the "religion reduces deviance" evidence were overwhelming, its public policy implications would remain unclear.

More broadly, what one might term "organic" exposure to religion or religious influences (for example, being born into a religious family, being unable to remember a time when you didn't attend church regularly, growing up surrounded by religious neighbors) needs to be distinguished from "intentional" exposure to religion (for example, joining a youth chapel's after-school sports league, being actively matched with a volunteer mentor from a religious organization, participating in a faith-based drug treatment program). Such evidence as we now have about how organic religion relates to socioeconomic outcomes under given conditions says nothing about the likely efficacy of intentional exposure to religion or the efficacy of faith-based programs.

Take, for example, drug treatment programs. Several faith-based drug treatment programs claim astonishing success rates. But we know that addicted persons are more likely to succeed in given types of drug treatment programs following several unsuccessful bouts of treatment. On average, do faith-based drug treatment programs attract a bigger pool of "down and out" or "last chance" persons who are on their nth treatment try? What about the fact that some faith-based drug treatment programs effectively require participants to "dry out," "get straight," or be "clean and sober" before officially entering the program?

What if it turned out that, even after controlling for such factors, the faith-based drug treatment programs' participants still relapsed at lower rates than otherwise comparable addicts? How best to conceptualize, measure, and isolate the "faith" in the "faith factor" as a main (or the main) determinant of the program's success? How might we do so across different types of faith-based programs—for example, the Salvation Army's semi-secular Adult Rehabilitation Centers versus, say, Teen Challenge's entirely Christ-centered ministries?

Alternatively, what if it turned out that, after doing the science right (or as right as humanly possible), the faith-based drug treatment programs' participants relapsed at rates equal to or even slightly higher than did otherwise comparable addicts in otherwise comparable secular programs? Would the faith-based programs then be a "failure"? What if the programs "failed" at the same rates, but the faith-based programs got the same sorry results for one-fifth the cost of the secular programs? One-half? Five-sixths?

Right now, all such questions remain to be answered. There has yet to be a single strongly experimental or quasi-experimental study of any major faith-based drug treatment program. Indeed, with respect to faith-based programs for drug addicts, prisoners, at-risk youth, and other populations, virtually everything one hears in the way of "success rates" are simple summary statistics based on dubious in-house data compiled by the religious organizations and ministries themselves.

Pluralistic

Too often, when pressed for hard data, yoked with secular or governmental partners in a common civic purpose, or required to compete for public resources by public rules, faith-based organizations balk.

In particular, certain evangelical Christian organizations seem to want to have it both ways. On the one hand, they are "all about" spirituality, salvation, and conversion. On the other hand, they claim—and often raise money through ads and direct mail appeals by claiming—that bringing troubled or needy people to accept Christ predictably and demonstrably lowers their probability of using drugs, doing crimes, and so on. But when it is time to prove the latter, they remind you that they are all about the former.

There is a difference between a pure altar-call ministry, an altar-call ministry in civic drag, and a genuine community-serving ministry in which sacred places work to achieve civic purposes. There is likewise a difference between taking private money from congenial donors of the same faith tradition, on the one side, and asking, on the other, that a pluralistic citizenry that includes Jews, Muslims, scores of other faith communities, and communities of non-believers, consider funding what may amount to nothing more than directly or indirectly tax-subsidized proselytizing.

I have absolutely no beef with a Reverend Billy Graham; he runs many major good-works ministries, domestic and international, but he knows what he is about, including the non-ecumenical, non-interfaith, impolitic proposition that all who do not accept Christ are lost unto eternity. Billy Graham and his ministries benefit from our pluralistic legal and constitutional traditions, and Graham himself has been so widely accepted as a principled national and global leader because he does not try to be all things to all people—or toward our government of, by, and for all people.

Let me state the case for respecting pluralism even more starkly: even if a given faith-based intervention were proven to be 100 percent effective, and even if it cost next to nothing to administer, it would still be wrong to have government promote or fund it if the intervention involved either tax-funded proselytizing, or involuntary adherence to or acceptance of a given religious orientation or tradition, or both.

I continue to hope and pray that, motivated by faith, America's godly people of diverse religious organizations and communities can and will dedicate themselves in common with other citizens to achieving important civic purposes. I continue to believe that the volunteer base of faith communities is deep enough, and that the hearts of religious volunteers are big enough, for community-serving ministries to tackle severe social and urban problems, to reach "the least of these," and to do so with a love and intensity that no strictly government or secular program can match. And I continue to profess government/secular partnerships with faith communities, and, more generally, the role of sacred places in achieving civic purposes, cannot advance if we tolerate legalized intolerance or bigotry toward religion in the public square.

But neither can these partnerships advance or last if, in our early eagerness to foster them, we bash secular outreach efforts, demean government-run social programs, overstate the efficacy of faith-based programs, shrug off the concerns of skeptics and secularists, and otherwise fail to witness what we profess to believe in truth, in grace, in true fellowship—and in effective civic action.

Endnotes

1 E. J. Dionne and John J. DiIulio, Jr., eds., *What's God Got to Do with the American Experiment?* (Washington, D.C.: Brookings Institution Press, 2000).

2 *Catechism of the Catholic Church*, Libreria Editrice Vaticana, 1997 English edition (New York: Image Book, 1997), p. 5.

3 Ram A. Cnaan, *Keeping Faith in the City: How 401 Religious Congregations Serve Their Neediest Neighbors*, Center for Research on Religion and Urban Civil Society, CRRUCS Report 2000-1, University of Pennsylvania, Philadelphia, Pennsylvania, March 20, 2000.

4 John J. DiIulio, Jr., "Black Churches," in Christopher H. Foreman, ed., *The African-American Predicament* (Washington, D.C.: Brookings Institution Press, 2000).

5 Byron Johnson, *A Better Kind of High: How Religious Commitment Reduces Drug Use Among Poor Urban Teens*, Center for Research on Religion and Urban Civil Society, CRRUCS Report 2000-2, University of Pennsylvania, Philadelphia, Pennsylvania, July 30, 2000.

CHAPTER ONE

Ryan Streeter

Introduction: Charitable Choice as Historical Phenomenon and Future Reality

In 1996, Congress passed the Personal Responsibility and Work Opportunity Reconciliation Act—or what is simply known as the welfare reform act. With it ended three decades of federal welfare conceived primarily in terms of cash assistance in favor of a work-based model. It has been heralded by advocates and opponents alike as one of the—if not the—most historically significant law passed in recent decades. Not only was the law a grand experiment in the devolution of authority for a major federal program to the states, it also signaled a shift in public opinion about the relationship of poverty, personal income, and work.

The law embodies the belief that low income individuals and families are better served in the long run by working than by receiving cash assistance. Work, not public subsidy in the form of welfare checks, is the track out of poverty.

The devolutionary nature of the law is based on the idea that states should be granted as much latitude as possible designing their own welfare-to-work system, because they best know how to tailor programs to their local economies, employers, public agencies, and economically troubled families. And because the road from welfare to work is often paved with many difficult challenges for individuals traveling along it, the law recognizes that religious organizations should be able to play a more active supportive role. The spiritual depth of their assistance is often the key to helping someone move out of poverty. If a local faith-based organization provides an effective service that complements, or rivals, the state or local government's effort to move families from public assistance into work, then that organization should be eligible to receive public funds for the service. Not only this, but the organizations should not be expected to denude their facilities and practices of all signs of their religious character. Except in cases of proselytization, religious instruction, and worship, public funds are lawfully permitted under the law's "Charitable Choice" provision to go to faith-based organizations. Immediately popular, Charitable Choice has found its way into additional federal bills pertaining to issues such as housing and crime, some of which have passed and others which are pending.

Charitable Choice signals a historically significant moment in the United States. In itself, it is a simple provision detailing the conditions by which federal funds may go to religious organizations. But as a sign of where we stand as a people, Charitable Choice is monumental. As a nation, E. J. Dionne points out in the pages that follow, we may be undergoing another period of renegotiation between the institutions of government and religious faith after a time of prolonged suspicion about the merits of faith in the public square. Dan Coats, who began to advocate for the increased participation of faith-based organizations in public welfare issues before it was popular, shows how long in coming this renegotiation has been. And legal scholar, Carl Esbeck, shows how far it has to go in order for the spirit and letter of the Charitable Choice provision to dance together harmoniously.

A more intimate relationship between religious and public institutions draws up some of our noblest sympathies for a strong, morally healthy public order and some of our greatest concerns that the spheres of church and state remain distinct, and thereby protected, from each other. In particular, Charitable Choice, which was designed primarily with assistance to the poor in our communities in mind, places us in this dilemma all the more. Can we afford to put church and state in closer cooperation? Can we, and especially those in need, afford not to?

Faith-based organizations, however, were not waiting for Charitable Choice to tell them it was okay to get into the social welfare business. Reports by the Independent Sector in 1988 and 1993 indicated, and research by Ram Cnaan, Robert Wineburg, and Stephanie Boddie has persuasively shown, that religious organizations were involved—in a substantial way—in the provision of social services already in the 1980s.[1] In many cases, local public officials and faith-based organizations had found ways to cooperate when their organizational purposes overlapped. Charitable Choice was therefore based upon emerging practices and not, as some have claimed, a merely idealized view of public partnership with the faith community.

But while the 1996 law did not introduce the faith community to welfare-related social service provision, it has apparently encouraged a wave of partnerships between government agencies and faith-based organizations. As Amy Sherman has discovered in her research, numerous partnerships have begun since 1996, indicating that the law has inspired their formation. In fact, in Sherman's recent nine-state study of new partnerships, 57 percent involved faith-based organizations with no previous history of collaboration with government. As she reports in these pages, the relationships are both financial and non-financial, and the financial collaborations include both large and, primarily, small contracts. In other words, not only has the law opened up service provision to a more diverse pool of providers—namely, faith-based organizations—but it has spawned an impressive range of contract sizes, as well. It is not only the large faith-based organizations that are getting the contracts.[2] But, as Stanley Carlson-Thies has shown, this wave of new collaboration is not without its problems. There exists widespread ignorance of Charitable Choice among public officials and faith community leaders. In some cases, there is downright resistance to opening up the contract bidding process to faith-based organizations. In his Charitable Choice Tracking Project, only one out of nine states, Texas, received a high passing grade for the way in which it has partnered with the faith community.

But all things considered, the interest in Charitable Choice has grown quickly in the several years it has been on the books. It has appeared in a number of bills proposed on Capitol Hill dealing with issues from crime to housing. Presidential candidates George W. Bush and Al Gore each devoted entire campaign speeches in 1999 to the increased involvement of the faith community in the public sector. President Bill Clinton followed in September 1999, when he spoke of an "emerging consensus" that faith-based organizations can provide an additional "leverage of the good things that the government is funding."[3] And since 1996, conferences on the role of faith-based organizations in publicly funded social welfare efforts have abounded. Government agencies have actively participated in the conference enthusiasm, including the U.S. Department

Phyllis Irene Bennett of Pennsylvania's Department of Public Welfare discusses the various ways in which public officials are reaching out to faith-based service providers in her state and across the nation.

of Health and Human Services, whose national conference on the subject in 1999 drew more than 300 people from across the country.

Most of the conferences have focused either upon the legitimacy of the idea of church-state collaboration or upon best practices or both. But until the April, 2000, Wingspread conference, "The Future of Government Partnerships with the Faith Community," no conference had brought together a select, diverse group of people to think strategically and practically about the future of these collaborations.

Co-sponsored by the Welfare Policy Center of Hudson Institute and the Johnson Foundation, the conference gathered 25 practitioners, academics, policy makers, and public officials to discuss ways to ensure a healthy future for government-faith partnerships. The conference did not debate whether the partnerships were legitimate. It held as its premise that such partnerships are allowable by law and, as such, should be set in their best light. Participants came well-prepared to think about the future.

The speeches during the conference take up the bulk of these proceedings. They are valuable contributions to the ongoing debate over the role of faith-based organizations in publicly funded human services. The discussion sparked by the speeches, which cannot be so easily transcribed, is summarized in these proceedings and thereby under-represented. Discussion was what the conference was about. It was lively and replete with wise and helpful suggestions for future practice. It is hoped that the summary in Chapter Eight, which was composed in part through the feedback from conference participants (but for which I take full responsibility), will lend some assistance to public and private sector leaders who have a stake in this issue.

Additionally, in Chapter Nine, three sets of recommendations follow the discussion summary. These recommendations are targeted toward public officials, faith leaders, and those researching and evaluating government-faith partnerships. Appearing together as they do, they are the first of their kind to appear in print anywhere. And for this reason, they should not be considered to be finished or doctrinaire. They should serve as guidelines for practitioners and catalysts for ongoing debate and discussion.

These proceedings are a fine mix of the big picture with the technical know-how of making government-faith partnerships work. E. J. Dionne, Dan Coats, and Don Eberly, whose speech was spontaneously invited at the conference's conclusion, cast this issue against the backdrop of American civil society and what it means for the future. Carl Esbeck, Stanley Carlson-Thies, and Amy Sherman draw attention to the issues that will make or break the future of government partnerships with the faith community. And together with suggestions for future practice made in the individual speeches, the discussion summary and the three sets of recommendations provide as solid a road map to the future as currently exists on this topic.

I would like to thank Chris Beem of The Johnson Foundation for his insight into and interest in this topic, and not only for hosting the conference but also for contributing significantly to its design. Thanks is also due to Curt Smith, Hudson Institute's Chief Operating Officer, for keeping the conference on time and on track through his role as moderator. The Johnson Foundation's Wendy Butler made the conference happen through her diligence and professional management of every detail, and Michael Philpy made these proceedings happen by transcribing and editing the speeches. And I would especially like to thank John DiIulio, prevented from attending the conference at the last minute in order to attend to an emergency, for taking time out of his extremely busy schedule to contribute an excellent Preface to this volume.

Endnotes

1 See *From Belief to Commitment: The Community Service Activities and Finances of Religious Congregations in the United States: Findings from a National Survey* (Washington, D.C.: Independent Sector, 1988 & 1993), and Ram Cnaan, Robert Wineburg, and Stephanie Boddie, *The Newer Deal: Social Work and Religion in Partnership* (New York: Columbia University Press, 1999), esp. 10 ff.

2 For the complete study that Sherman cites in her speech, see Amy Sherman, *The Growing Impact of Charitable Choice: A Catalogue of New Collaborations Between Government and Faith-Based Organizations in Nine States* (Washington, D.C.: The Center for Public Justice, 2000).

3 Speech at the White House Prayer Breakfast, September 28, 1999 (Washington, D.C.: Federal Document Clearing House, 1999).

Religion's Third Renegotiation with the Public Square

The question concerning the extent to which religion and politics should have any-thing to do with each other is quickly becoming a very practical issue. Partnerships between government agencies and religious organizations in numerous states are increasing. Yet, this issue also involves some of the most fundamental questions about the meaning of our country, the meaning of our Constitution, and how we look at ourselves. This, I think, explains both why there is such great interest in this issue and why the issue creates such fierce argument.

One view concentrates on America's pluralistic and secular Constitution that has promoted freedom, diversity, and oddly, the very strength of American religious communities. A state independent of organized religion has been freedom's, and reli-gion's, finest friend. A central motivation for the creation of free and tolerant institu-tions was a desire to end wars over God and religion.

In the other account, freedom itself is rooted in a theistic—many would say Judeo-Christian—commitment to the inviolable dignity of the individual human being. This belief arises, in the words of the Declaration of Independence, from "the Law of nature and Nature's God." A belief in God places healthy restraints on the human tendency to deify political systems or individual political strongmen—and insists that even strongmen are accountable to a Higher Authority.

This argument is as old as our republic, and I do not know if we will be any more successful now than in the past in resolving it. As Alan Wolfe has written, "Two hundred years after the brilliant writings of Madison and Jefferson on the topic, Americans cannot make up their minds whether religion is primarily private, public, or some uneasy combination of the two."

I think it is also important to acknowledge that we Americans can be quite inconsistent in our views of how and when religion should influence politics. Many who welcome the prophetic role of the churches in movements to abolish slavery, promote civil rights, and secure social justice are skeptical of applying religion's prophetic voice to matters such as abortion, sexuality, or family life. Many who wel-come the second set of commitments can be just as wary of crusades rooted in a social gospel.

In his autobiography, the Reverend Jerry Falwell was admirably candid in acknowledging the contrast between his reaction to church-based civil rights activists in 1965 ("Preachers are not called upon to be politicians but to preach the gospel," he said then) and his later embrace of political activism in response to the Supreme Court's 1973 decision legalizing abortion.

Today, the issue of religion's involvement in public life has grabbed a central place in current political debate. The two leading presidential candidates, George W. Bush and Al Gore, are talking enthusiastically about what government can do to help "faith-based organizations" solve social problems. At a White House prayer breakfast last year, President Clinton embraced what he called "an emerging consensus about the ways in which faith organizations and our government can work together." Pastors dealing with social problems are landing on the covers of national magazines and scholars are predicting a new "great awakening" of religious fervor in the country.

The turn of the millennium in America may well be remembered as a time when the country renegotiated the relationship between religion and public life, faith and culture. We are not about to chuck religious freedom, impose censorship or herd everyone into a church, synagogue or mosque. Indeed, it is partly because of advances in religious freedom—the result of court decisions and cultural changes that occurred during the 1960s—that it is even possible to talk about increased cooperation between the worlds of faith and government. There is no consensus yet on how church and state are supposed to work together, let alone how much. This is nothing new. Arguments for strong barriers between religion and government have waxed and waned through American history, for radically different reasons in different times.

It is important to understand the political context of this issue's origins. In the late '70s, Nathan Glazer called the newly developing religious right a "defensive offensive" meant not to create a kind of theocracy but to restore the consensus on values that existed—or at least seemed to exist—before the '60s. On the other, those dismayed by the religious right saw them trying to tear down barriers between Church and State, thereby threatening religious liberty.

One of the openings, I think, for consensus right now can be seen in the way that many rank-and-file evangelical Christians have been as turned off as the rest of the country by polarization around political issues related to religion. "There's a certain backlash against the shrill, partisan message they've heard," according to Nathan Hatch, the provost at Notre Dame and a historian of evangelical Christianity. "A lot of Evangelicals are suburban people, and they much more easily identify with a

George Bush than a Jerry Falwell or a Gary Bauer. They're people of values. They're also tolerant."

As we try to understand the array of opinion concerning faith and government's relationship, we can be helped a lot by Bill Galston's description of Americans as "tolerant traditionalists." Perhaps we could say that when people err on this issue, they are ignoring one of the pieces of that formulation. Tolerant traditionalism is a difficult position to maintain, and some might argue that it is philosophically an inconsistent view. But most Americans do not see it that way. The consensus that we seem to be groping for comes out of this tolerant traditionalist impulse.

I think this conference should be understood as a contribution to what might be called the third stage in a long national debate.

What we might term a period of "white Protestant hegemony in America"—the first stage—began to erode with the end of Prohibition, arguably the last political project to unite mainline and evangelical Protestants. This, together with the

Brookings Institution senior fellow and Washington Post columnist E. J. Dionne addresses the conference participants as Stanley Carlson-Thies looks on.

Scopes trial—as Terry Eastland has pointed out—Al Smith's presidential candidacy, and a new urban-based Democratic coalition formed around the New Deal that included Catholics, Jews, and African Americans, marked a very strong cultural change.

This led to a second stage in the '60s which involved a hard push for separation (sometimes from Protestants themselves), as reflected in many of the relevant court decisions during that time. It was when the civil rights movement became a very powerful force in our nation's life. It was when John F. Kennedy's election as president marked the full entry of Roman Catholics into the mainstream of American life. That era sought to right historic wrongs done to African Americans, sweep away long-standing barriers to Jews, effectively end restrictive covenants and initiate new movements to defend the rights of Latinos and Asians. All brought the pervasively white and Protestant ethos in government-financed institutions and society into question.

Today's commotion is rooted in a new fear—that the combination of legal decisions and cultural trends has marginalized religion more than is either necessary for religious freedom or desirable for the country. In creating what Yale Law School professor Stephen Carter called "The Culture of Disbelief" in his book of that title, the country seemed to replace old prejudices (of race and religion) with a new prejudice against belief itself.

The current renegotiation of boundaries—the third stage—has already borne fruit. In 1995, new federal guidelines to school administrators were designed to make clear that while the state cannot impose religion, students cannot be forced to be secular against their will or silenced in their personal expressions of religion.

The possibility that a new consensus on these matters exists is further evidenced by the Clinton administration's issuance in 1997 of guidelines requiring government supervisors to respect individual expressions of faith by religious employees. Christians could keep Bibles on their desks, Muslim women could wear scarves, Jewish workers' schedules should be accommodated so that they could observe holy days, and so on. This might seem like common sense, but they reflect a new awareness that preserving religious freedom entails both keeping government out of the way and protecting the free expression of believers. In a sense, government policy is struggling to honor both religion clauses of the First Amendment.

The battle over expanded government aid to faith-based institutions will not be so easy, which is why meetings like this are so very useful. Melissa Rogers, of the Baptist Joint Committee on Public Affairs, calls it "the wrong way to do right." She means that the admirable efforts by faith-based charities should get much more private and corporate support, but not government help. Yet Gore's endorsement of "Charitable Choice" suggests a slow shifting of the boundaries being drawn by moderate and even liberal Democrats who have come to see the churches as indispensable allies to government in solving problems.

To characterize the new discussion in what some might see as an excessively optimistic light, it does appear that many among devout believers are more sensitive than their forebears might have been to the demands of religious pluralism and tolerance; and that many Americans inclined toward secularism are more alive now than they were even a decade ago to the contributions made by religious people and institutions to social renewal. "The role of government at all levels is being redefined, but so is the role of religion. We must find new ways to think about the relationship of religion and public life," Jim Wind of the Alban Institute has said. There is also an opening toward a more nuanced understanding of the interaction between religious commitment and social change, between personal transformation and social justice. This is a tricky question that goes to the heart of this debate. "Religion's chief contribution to morality is to enable people to transform their lives," James Q. Wilson writes. "Faith can only transform one person at a time, and then only as the result of the personal attention of one other person." Patrick Glynn, of the Institute for Communitarian Policy Studies, makes a powerful parallel point. "Religion does its real work in politics not by arousing moral indignation, but by awakening the individual conscience," he writes. "The distinction is a subtle but important one. Moral indignation drives us to condemn others; conscience prompts us to question ourselves."

We still need to get at the question of what the relationship is between individual transformation and the broader quest for social justice. In Glynn's terms, conscience may prompt individuals to change their own behavior and also prompt them to become agents of social change. The work of Saul Alinsky, which continues through the Industrial Areas Foundation is very much about this dialectic between individual transformation and the push faith affords people to seek social change. This is a very important issue that we need to put on the table for further discussion.

Charitable Choice, the provision of the 1996 welfare reform act that permits religious organizations to receive contracts, vouchers, and other government funding, presents additional challenges.

Charitable Choice has largely been supported by conservatives and opposed by liberals—with some important exceptions such as Sen. Paul Wellstone of Minnesota. But that is only part of the story. A 1998 survey of 1,236 religious congregations by Mark Chaves of the University of Arizona found that the law may prove of far more benefit to the more liberal congregations. "Politically conservative congregations are much less likely to apply for government funds than are middle-of-the-road or liberal congregations," Chaves found. He also reported that predominantly African American congregations are "very substantially more likely to be willing to apply for government funds than are white congregations." While scholars like Amy Sherman may have some differences with this data, the study nonetheless suggests the possible distortions in trying to understand faith-based programs if they are only seen through the lens of "liberalism and conservatism." As Chaves notes, "If Charitable Choice initiatives are successful in reaching American congregations, the congregations most likely to take advantage of them may not be the ones our political and religious leaders expect to take advantage of them."

Making Charitable Choice work remains an enormous challenge because constitutional worries about the free exercise of religion cannot be lightly dismissed.

Seen from the perspective of religious groups, there is the danger that entanglement with government will require them to weaken or water down their faith commitments, no matter how strongly the law tilts in their favor. I was recently at a meeting in which leaders from a gospel mission were aligning with Americans United for the Separation of Church and State because of their fears of the strings possibly attached to government aid.

Seen from the perspective of those fearful of intimate ties between government and religion, there is legitimate worry that supporting the religious groups with the highest success rates will entail government aid to precisely those organizations that require the strongest level of religious commitment from participants. Some scholars suggest that spiritually demanding programs appear to produce the best results. Those who fear that government support of religiously based charities could move quickly into "excessive entanglement" with religion can cite the most optimistic research on the success of such programs to justify their concerns. Government aid, if distributed on the basis of which programs work best, might go disproportionately to the religiously based programs that raise the most difficult First Amendment issues. This goes to the heart of the debate and needs to be continuously addressed.

There are other areas that we need to explore as well. There are ways that faith organizations can be helped that would not hurt too many people. I have said before that we may soon have a church in America called "Saint 501(c)(3)." It is a legitimate question to ask what, if anything, is lost when a congregation runs its social programs through a separate nonprofit organization.

The argument over government aid sometimes gets us away from another argument we need to have. There exists an enormous reluctance on the part of corporate philanthropy to support the work of faith-based organizations. A lot of corporations act as if they are under the First Amendment—rules under which they do not need to live.

James Q. Wilson has suggested that we "facilitate the movement of private funds into church-connected enterprises." He has called for a kind of religious "United Way." I have found that a lot of people could come together around this idea. It is not a trivial idea or an evasion of larger issues to say that the private corporate sector could be doing much more to help religious organizations. The truth is that these organizations always will—and always should—rely primarily on private support. This is an issue that is too little explored, and gatherings such as this could help it gain momentum.

As a country, we are terribly torn about what religion-in-public should mean. Collectively, we seem suspicious of politicians who are too religious, and suspicious of politicians who are not religious at all. This can lead to the very worst forms of religious expression. As Gregg Easterbrook writes in his recent book, *Beside Still Waters*: "If a politician or celebrity stands up to mumble about being blessed by the Lord, and speaks in a manner unmistakably vacuous and intended for public consumption, nobody minds. If the same person says with conviction, I really believe my faith requires me to do this or that, the expression will be condemned as inappropriate." The paradoxes of religious faith are obvious. It can create community, and it can divide communities. It can lead to searing self-criticism, and it can promote a pompous self-satisfaction. It can encourage dissent and conformity, generosity and narrow-mindedness. It can engender both righteous behavior and self-righteousness.

Its very best and very worst forms can be inward-looking. Religion's finest hours have been the times when intense belief led to social transformation, yet some of its darkest days have entailed the translation of intense belief into the ruthless imposition of orthodoxy.

I suggest a few matters for further discussion as you continue to explore these ideas over the course of the conference.

The first is that to which I alluded earlier. If the most successful programs that are also those demanding the greatest religious commitment, what is government to do about that? And what is the response of the supporters of faith-based organizations to those in the separationist camp that wish these groups well but have, I think, legitimate constitutional worries?

A second issue is to what extent voucherized programs get in the way—rather than expand—national networks in areas we think we need them. This is, if you will, an explicitly liberal question, because when you come to areas such as creating networks of pre-school or after-school programs, there will be a great debate in coming years as to whether or not voucherizing these programs might prevent the creation of national models and the spread of needed programs around the country. The other side will argue legitimately, especially with respect to after-school programs, that we have extensive networks that we do not want to break off, and vouchers would be essential to preserving these networks. It is important to look forward to new areas—such as the pre- and after-school issues about which we will soon have great national debate—where the choice between broad networks and vouchers presents us with some serious policy questions, all constitutional questions aside.

Third, I would like to place on the table the question about limits of the state. I do not think that this discussion requires one to believe that state-run programs have been universal failures. The rhetoric of this movement turns off lots of people like me (who do not believe the era of big government is over). The rhetoric that has faith-based organizations replacing a whole lot of government programs has a tendency to make people like me ask, does this mean Social Security is a failure? Medicare? Medicaid? There are a lot of government efforts on which these other efforts depend. Were the government programs knocked out of the picture, faith-based organizations would be overwhelmed with new problems to solve. I think it is worth debating to what extent faith-based organizations replace government activities and to what extent they supplement them. This is a legitimate political debate. There are areas where replacement is conceivable, others where it is not, and this creates an issue around which we will continue to have fierce debates.

Two final points. As stated earlier, the "St. 501(c)(3)" issue is one for which we need more and better thinking. We would do well to continue the debate on this point.

Lastly, we need much tougher evaluations and assessments of these programs. Amy Sherman has located some programs that might be subjected to these kinds of assessments, and it would be good to design evaluations to carry out on them. Someone has once said that the plural of anecdote is not data. What we have in this area are programs that are so popular, and people want so much for them to work, that there is a natural human tendency to say, "yes, these work," without subjecting them to the kind of tough evaluation to which government programs have been subjected.

I close with the words of the historian Richard Fox, who wrote of the power of religion in our public life. He says that it is "both a democratic social power—a capacity to build community—and as a tragic perspective that acknowledges the perennial failing of human beings to make community endure."

"Religion," Fox continues, "allows people to grapple with the human mysteries that neither science nor politics can address. But it also provides a force that science and politics can call on in their effort to understand and transform the social world." I think that helps explain why we are gathering here and why people across the country are engaged in this work. I wish all of you well in your endeavors.

The Purpose of Government's Partnership with Faith-Based Organizations

I want to thank Curt Smith, Ryan Streeter, and Jay Hein at Hudson Institute for convening what I think is an important meeting of some important people on an important topic. And I really wish you success in thinking through and defining how we can best proceed in the implementation of Charitable Choice and do it in a way that is successful.

Don Eberly points out in his latest essay, "Compassionate Conservatism," how extraordinarily far we have come in the public arena in regard to the whole idea of faith-based organizations engaging in what was formerly the exclusive purview of a centralized state operation, and how much the dialogue has changed. And that caused me to think back on my involvement in this debate. It first started in the early eighties when I joined a renegade band of liberals and conservatives to form the Select Committee on Children and Family in the House of Representatives back in 1983. Our goal was to try to get a group of House members to pull together the oversight of these issues. At the time jurisdiction over issues that affected children and the family was distributed over thirteen different House committees, and we wanted to centralize the focus in one committee. Our purpose was to identify the problem, analyze where government was, and make recommendations to those various committees.

We used our first year for fact-finding. We held hearings in Washington and across the country. We visited numerous sites and met with care providers to learn of the state of children and families in America and inquire into how they were dealing with the problems in their communities. Almost exclusively, the hearings and the meetings were designed to address the government's role. The experts came before us, and virtually 95 percent of them said, "We have this and that government program, and this one doesn't work as well as it should, we need more money here, we need more governmental effort there, we need more guidance from Washington," and so on. It became very disconcerting because of the disconnect between the dysfunction that we found everywhere in terms of broken families and broken lives, substance abusers, and juvenile delinquents, etc., and the proliferation of government efforts to try to address those problems. This disconnect was growing at a magnitude that was difficult to get our arms around and to fully comprehend. Problems were growing, and government's ever-increasing effort was not making a substantive or quantitative difference.

Near the end of this first year, I was overwhelmed with facts and statistics about social dysfunctions and was totally discouraged about the ability of government to provide an adequate response. I began to search for a better answer. I remember praying for God's help after leaving Salt Lake City where we spent a day with the Mormon community and realized that if they couldn't make their government services work, given all their emphasis on family and service to people, how could the rest of us?

Two remarkable things happened. The first happened when we traveled to Orange County, California, to visit a model juvenile rehabilitation facility, which was the best effort that the federal government, the state of California, and Orange County could put together. They had decided to create *the* model for juvenile rehabilitation. They had a federal grant, state grant, local money; they had the very best facilities. They hired the best people from all over the country and were able to pay top salaries. We sat down for breakfast around the table, and they told us about their programs and hopes for successful rehabilitation of the troubled youths they were serving. Following breakfast, we met separately with groups of ten of the juveniles in the facility. We spent an hour talking to those young people, and asking the question: Is what's happening here making a difference in your life? When you leave this program, is your life going to be any different? Person after person after person said that nothing had changed. "When I go out, I'm going right back to the same situation." Do you think you'll go back to doing drugs? "I don't want to, but I probably will." Do you think you'll go back to crime? "Well, yeah probably."

So, I left very discouraged and met Congressman Frank Wolf, who was also very discouraged. And as we were standing there talking about all of this, a voice interrupted us from behind. It was one of the young people there who was not in either of our groups. He was sixteen years old. He asked if we were Congressmen, and we told him we were. He said, "My name is George. I'm in this program here and I imagine that what you've heard has made you discouraged." And we said, "Yeah, we're very discouraged." He replied, "Well, I wanted to say something to you just so you didn't leave here without hope. I'm leaving here in two weeks, and I'm leaving with great hope for the future. I'm going to go back to my family and try to help pull that family together. I'm going to go back to school and get my high school degree. I have plans to go to college and get my college degree. I want to meet someone that I can marry and be the mother of my children. And I'm looking forward to getting a job, and I just have great hope for the future." We just stood there in amazement, and I asked him, "George, what makes you different than everyone else we've talked to?" He said, "Well, two months ago a person from a prison ministry came and talked to me. My life has been transformed by the message that person gave me and the hope that I now have through my faith about the future."

The second thing that happened occurred a week later, when we had a hearing in Macon, Georgia, about the plight of rural youth. And the thirteenth and last witness was a black minister from the Macedonian Missionary Church of Waycross, Georgia. We had just completed three hours of testimony from the "experts"—all calling for more federal dollars and more federal intervention. Then this humble minister said in a soft-spoken but eloquent manner, "What you Congresswomen and men don't seem to get and what you don't hear from the people that talk to you is this: All your government programs that have come down into my town have failed, because they failed to recognize that every human being is not only mind and body, but soul and spirit. I deal with problems with rural youth, mostly minority youth, and we have every problem that you can imagine. And your government programs don't treat the whole person. If you don't treat the soul and spirit along with mind and body, you are doomed to failure. You may provide a roof over someone's head, and you may provide food for someone to eat, and you may provide some kind of structured training program, but unless you change the heart, unless you address the matters of soul and spirit, you're not going to be successful. Now, government can't do that. You're trying to make people whole, but you're only addressing half the problem. There's a rightful place for what you do, but there's also a rightful place for institutions like the church, institutions like the family, institutions like the community that can bring forth a faith perspective to solve the problem. And until you find a way to link what the government is doing to what the faith community is doing, in a way that successfully addresses the needs but also nourishes the soul, you are not going to solve the problem."

That was the genesis of a lot of effort and study that culminated—through the great help of Curt Smith, his staff, and others on my staff—in the Project for American Renewal. This was a set of fifteen initiatives that government could undertake under the three categories of Effective Compassion, Community Empowerment, and Fathering, Mentoring, and Family. We had several goals. The first goal wasn't to enact legislation, but rather to create a dialogue in Congress on the role of faith-based institutions in helping the process of devolution away from government to the local and state levels. We wanted to do our part in promoting the use of mediating institutions in the restoration of civil society. And, frankly, we wanted to at least begin a dialogue within my party that conservatism meant more than economic freedom but also included utilizing private sector, faith-based institutions that would not only feed the body, but touch the soul.

In a way, we were trying to articulate a third way, a new alternative to what most were viewing at that time as a failed government solution. Many were saying the free market's not going to solve this problem: we have a serious breakdown in the civil society of this country and a moral dilemma as well as an economic dilemma. And we need to address that, and we need to do that through the use of mediating institutions. As Don Eberly pointed out, we don't really realize how far we've come, particularly in terms of changing the dialogue. Everyone in this room, at this table, and others who aren't here have played a major role in that. I played a small part in the Congressional level, but you and those in your communities have played the major role.

Sometimes we fail to stop and notice that a remarkable transformation has taken place within the public sector, in terms of how it views the roles of faith-based organizations and mediating institutions and how it views its own role. Just the fact that we're having this conference makes the point. Just the fact that someone as prominent as E. J. Dionne would come and speak to this issue is testimony to the level of progress this topic has made. Just the fact that many from both parties are now talking about, not whether there is a role for this, but how we make it work, is very significant. This is a very significant accomplishment, almost a miracle, and we ought to celebrate that.

Now, when we developed the Project for American Renewal, we had some real concerns. Obviously, we were concerned about the establishment clause. But we were also concerned that we might be limiting the real transforming work of faith-based institutions by linking them to government in a way that circumscribed them so much that their missions were compromised. We were concerned about the capacity of civil society and the faith-based communities to address the scope of the problem. We were concerned about the accountability and the administrative ability of these organizations. And so we emphasized tax credits, primarily the charity tax credits, as a way to kick-start some of these efforts through demonstration projects. And then we focused upon grants for demonstration projects in order to highlight the impact and the effectiveness of these organizations, rather than try to establish legislative-based government response.

Out of all this, the Renewal Alliance was established, consisting of a group of Senate and House members who were committed to these principles. The House members brought some of the economic empowerment and educational choice initiatives to that alliance, and the Senate incorporated many of the educational and family building initiatives from the Project for American Renewal. Today, the

Renewal Alliance is still going strong under the leadership of Rick Santorum in the Senate, and J. C. Watts and Joe Pitts in the House. So there are initiatives underway. But the real legislative initiative, which is also the basis for this conference, was John Ashcroft's Charitable Choice provision in the welfare reform act.

I have a certain ambivalence about Charitable Choice because I was very concerned about some of the things that I've mentioned before—about the establishment clause impact and how that program might be administered. Senator Ashcroft was able to secure some language that retained the distinctive religious atmosphere of faith-based organizations and work through the Title 7 discrimination language issues in terms of hiring. But to do so we needed to include a prohibition on religious instruction and proselytization. There's a very fine balance that we're trying to walk here in terms of allowing these faith-based institutions to provide services for people that need them, and yet not take away the essence of what made them so successful, which is the faith-based component. That's really what you're all about, and I commend that. The process of developing a framework, which Hudson is attempting to facilitate here, in order to walk this balance beam successfully is, I think, extraordinarily important.

One of the things that I very much worried about when we first put this Project of American Renewal together, which I also worried about with regard to Charitable Choice, was

Former U.S. Senator Dan Coats describes for the group the journey that led him to launch the Project for American Renewal, a large-scale effort aimed at empowering community-redeeming organizations.

that we would not do it successfully. This, we knew, would provide fuel for many who have been wedded strictly to government solutions to say, "See! We told you all that you didn't have the capacity to handle the problem. You have a series of missteps and mistakes and abuses." We did not want so easily to retreat back into the government-centric model. So it's critically important that we make this work, critically important that we develop a framework and a code of conduct to which these organizations can adhere. The evangelical church community developed the Evangelical Council for Financial Accountability, which is a financial accountability group that gives a stamp of approval to organizations that adhere to a prescribed set of high standards. I think this is very important to do wherever there is the potential for harmful mistakes or an abuse of privileges. When we put public money into the hands of private entities, we have got to be sure that the money is used in the proper setting, we have got to make sure results are demonstrated. So analysis and accountability are both fundamental to the success that we need.

Now, there are flirtations with a number of initiatives in the Congress, although we are currently in a year where people are doing the bare minimum required to get elected and then set up new administrations—so I don't expect a lot to happen. But, for instance, the Elementary and Secondary Education Act (ESEA) includes language that essentially would allow for the safe and drug-free schools portion of the act to deal with faith-based groups in the communities. There's concern that the Charitable Choice prescriptions for welfare don't immediately fit with these other programs. Already, we've learned that Senator Kennedy is seriously thinking about offering an amendment to the ESEA in the Senate that would take out the anti-discrimination clause. So you run the risk now of rushing to do a good thing, but in rushing to impose this on more federal programs, we're really retreating from analysis before we have a good test of whether or not it's working.

I think it's very important to make sure that we know which organizations are the recipients of these funds, that we analyze how successful their programs are, and we document that success. All this means time, and all this means effort, but I think it's very important to establish the success of these programs before we expand Charitable Choice to other federally funded initiatives. This is important for a couple of reasons, but most important, I think, is that demonstrated success at the current scope of services lays the groundwork for a broader effort that Don Eberly would call a remoralization of America—that is, addressing some of the moral issues that go well beyond the delivery of services in welfare reform.

In one sense, they are parallel tracks in that some moral renewal is taking place outside of the government sector, but in another sense, the failure of the one could negatively impact the other. The success of Charitable Choice, in terms of successfully integrating the faith-based model, impacts the elements of remoralization such as character development, accountability, personal responsibility, the importance of the family structure, and the importance of faith. This is because, in a sense, we are bringing more than just the check, more than just the service into the equation. And to the extent that we can see renewal, or remoralization, within the more limited framework of the delivery of those services, it can be the basis for a lot of other good things outside of the government model that would promote a rebuilding of the moral framework and the role of civil society in America.

A lot of this effort has to take place outside of the government effort and outside of the legislative effort. The Project for American Renewal was designed to show success in some of these areas, not to create a federal model or a state model meant to address renewal comprehensively. It was a governmental complement to a wider effort aimed at inspiring non-government, private, volunteer, and nonprofit, faith-based initiatives to spring up all across America and in all kinds of different forms.

As some of you probably know, I'm now serving as the president of National Big Brothers/Big Sisters. We have two initiatives which I'm very excited about, one of which is a pilot program in five major inner-city, mostly minority churches. Many of you are aware of Floyd Flake's efforts at Allen AME Church in Jamaica, Queens. That was one of our pilot projects along with Detroit, St. Louis, Jacksonville, Florida, and Indianapolis, Indiana. With these pilot projects, in terms of providing mentors (we have a 100-year history of providing mentors), you could rate the work of Big Brothers/Big Sisters from an accountability standpoint—that is, are we making it work? From a practical standpoint, we wanted to integrate our work with the inner-city churches in providing volunteers to the minority community. A long list of African-American, Hispanic, and other minority children are waiting for mentors because a very short list of adult minority volunteers qualified to be mentors. And working through these churches is a wonderful way to attract responsible volunteers, as well as bringing the faith-based element into the effort. The churches provide a wonderful source of mentors that can really help impact lives for the better.

The second thing is just in the fledgling stage of Big Brothers/Big Sisters, and John DiIulio has helped get it started. John and our CEO have talked about incorporating our organizational efforts into the Prison Fellowship program to serve children of prisoners. They have a program with which they need structure and organization and some help in lessons that we've learned in our 100 years of providing mentoring. It's a very exciting prospect. We are working with inner-city churches and Prison Fellowship in a very significant way. And, we plan to carefully monitor and measure the results with help from Public-Private Ventures. Accountability and measured results are keys to the program.

In conclusion, here at the dawn of the new millennium we ought to be very hopeful and full of optimism, because the centralized, bureaucratic, only-Washington-can-do-it mentality of the past three or four decades has been successfully challenged and, in a bipartisan way, people are beginning to think about different models. The first instinct is no longer to first call a Congressman or find some other direct link to Washington in the belief that it is the only place where solutions can be found. And across America you see promising initiatives—the Indianapolis Front Porch Alliance and all the many dozens of initiatives which each of you can name and which can take place without government support, without government initiative, and without a federalized or state-controlled apparatus. That is exciting. I think we ought to feel very, very good about that.

We have to realize, secondly, that the door is open to the restoration of faith-based, volunteer, community, nonprofit initiatives that can address some of our most serious social needs, restore communities, and restore families. Third, we can't discount the challenge ahead or the scope of the problem. I think that it was terribly destructive to these mediating institutions when we usurped so much of their authority and so many of their resources, over such a long period of time. The fact is, it's going to take a lot to rebuild this infrastructure. We have to realize that we must find ways to make this successful, or the retreat to government is inevitable. You can already hear the cry, you can just see the images on the news, you can just hear the speeches on the floor of the House and the Senate about problems that are not being addressed, about failure and abuses of this new effort to address the problem.

Fourth, this conference is important because it is focused on establishing a framework to make this work. I would urge you, once you get beyond the rhetoric of people like me, to get down to the hard work of establishing guidelines for accountability, guidelines for success, and putting a framework together that can be implemented across the board. It is an extremely important function, and necessary for our success. Fifth, and finally, if we are successful in this, we can set the stage for what I would call a broader moral renewal through the role of these mediating institutions and nongovernment efforts in addressing a moral revolution, a moral regeneration in our society.

So, I'm thankful for the opportunity to play a small role in this and thankful for the opportunity to be associated with Hudson. I've established a foundation through Hudson called the Foundation for American Renewal. I established this out of the conviction that if we're serious about initiatives that don't rely on government, and that avoid entanglement in the many restrictions that might come with partnering with government, then it is important that we are actively providing alternative ways of supporting these initiatives. I thought the best way to use my unused campaign funds was to continue the Project for American Renewal by creating a Foundation for American Renewal. It is in the fledgling stage, but it's located at Hudson and Ryan Streeter and Curt Smith are directly involved in helping me figure out how to do this and make it successful.

We need to look for funding resources. We need to energize the philanthropic past of American society in providing the necessary support for this. The store-front, low-rent, low salary operations can only go so far. And if we want to attract the right kind of people, in which we operate the right kind of programs, we have to provide the resources for them. I am connected with an initiative called the National Heritage

Foundation which now has enrolled over five thousand private foundations all dedicated to charitable efforts where people will take their own money or fund raise to establish a charity that works directly with local missions of their own choosing. It might be addressing drug abuse in junior high, it might be addressing homelessness, it might be addressing teen pregnancy, it might be addressing behavioral trouble in the neighborhood, it might be addressing scholarships for underprivileged children, and any number of other social needs. It's exciting to be a part of that and see the growth of these foundations. We are trying to initiate Congressional District Foundations, one in every Congressional district in the country. There are two purposes in this. When someone comes to their Congressman and asks, "What are we going to do about this?" Instead of the Congressman saying, "Well, we've got this or that federal program," or "Maybe I can get an amendment in," the Congressman can say, "You know, we have an organization here in this district that is dedicated to the purpose of addressing these very types of problems. I'm supporting these kinds of initiatives and recommend that you talk to this person over here who can help you take the initiative in responding to this problem."

A secondary purpose of the Congressional District Foundation is to use it as a basis for acquainting members of Congress with the power and effectiveness of these organizations. So when Congress debates the role of nongovernment, faith-based solutions, members can point to the success of initiatives in their districts with which they have a personal knowledge. Or, when legislation to enact a charity tax credit is offered, they will recognize the value of incentives to empower people as opposed to empowering government.

These are just two examples of the types of things that need to take place to provide funding for local solutions to social problems. We don't always want to have to go to Washington or the state capitals and simply say, "We can't make this work unless you fund it." Inevitably it will be tied to restrictions that can potentially undermine the very essence of what these organizations are trying to accomplish.

I hope I've been of some encouragement to what all of you are doing in this conference. I trust that what you do here will extend beyond this conference to help ensure that we stay on the right track and keep moving forward. If we continue making the progress we're making, we're going to be a witness to an extraordinary transformation of civil society.

I think it would be helpful to bring back the commission that we received from Ryan Streeter in his letter. Ryan made the observation that little attention has been given to designing optimal ways to facilitate and sustain the necessary cooperation between faith-based organizations and the government. And we're to give some concrete results to that goal. He said that the hope would be that something would be published by way of conference proceedings as a set of recommendations to policy makers and community leaders—and I would add civil servants, like Phyllis Bennett here, who are working in the trenches, and then the people who are actually operating the faith-based organizations as well.

And one of the issues that Ryan said we need to talk about is the proper legal framework, and of course, this is the session to talk about that framework. Before I jump into just law as such, I thought I'd first give some disclosures. First, I am a Christian. I converted to Christianity at the age of 25 as I was wrapping up my legal studies in Ithaca, New York, at Cornell and of course, that does frame my worldview. Second, I believe in the separation of church and state. The legal principle is found in the establishment clause of the First Amendment. The clause is a codification of the recognition that the nation's Constitution has deregulated religion. That's what it recognizes. We deregulate those things that are inherently religious. We took the government out of that specific activity. And we are a nation of laws, we have the world's first written constitution, and it's our obligation to honor that.

Third, I believe that social welfare that works best ends not at delivery of services, but at changing lives. Now, by changing one's life I mean how one views herself, values herself, perceives herself as capable of parenting, of doing meaningful work, of all the indicators of flourishing in life. So, welfare that works best means changing lives.

Fourth, I believe that spiritually rich faith-based organizations are not the only organizations capable of facilitating the life changes of the recipients of welfare. I think it's really arrogant to ignore the very fine work done by some secular providers, as well as by government itself, in the direct delivery of services.

Nonetheless, while justified more by anecdotes than hard, empirical research, faith-based organizations appear to be, on average, more successful service providers. And there are at least three reasons (there are, no doubt, more reasons) that, over time, have come to my attention—none of which are very surprising.

First, the faith-based organization (FBO) has deep roots in the communities where the people who are most using the services live. These organizations are in the inner urban settings, and they are often the only organization that hasn't left, the only institution that has remained on site. They have high credibility with the people who are there. They have high access to the people who are there. They have themselves a very high stake in the area. For if these communities totally collapse, the faith-based organizations, the church and synagogues and so on, will themselves close and be gone. So, it's an advantage of location, credibility, access, and high personal stake that gets a successful outcome.

Second, there is a quality difference in the services that are rendered. Now again, I don't want to take away from secular providers and the government delivering services themselves, but on average, and over the long-haul there is a quality difference. You can look at secular programs and faith-based organizations and they may be delivering seemingly the same goods and services, they may have similar delivery mechanisms, organizational strategies; if you look at their organizational charts they just look like any other group. And yet, nonetheless, FBOs have different motivations, they perceive differently the people they're trying to help and their worth, and they desire different outcomes. You can express that in terms of the word *holistic* or whatever. There is a different quality, a better quality.

Third, that much depends on how you define, or who you put under the category of, "faith-based organizations." If you include a church-affiliated group that is still pretty secular and groups that are intensely or richly religious, then you may put all those under the heading of faith-based organizations, as I would. Some of those, perhaps not a majority, have a major orientation toward conversion. Call it proselytizing, evangelism, whatever label you want to put on it. And of course, that has two aspects. If the person receiving services is in fact persuaded, and becomes a convert, that gives him a new set of motivations, foundations, principles from which to work on his problem, be it a drug addiction, or crime, or battering a spouse, or whatever. But it also gives the employees of the faith-based organization and their volunteers a different motivation, a motivation of conversion. Conversion is a very powerful motivator.

Those are three differences, and one of the questions we have to struggle with is: Is it desirable to compartmentalize points one and two, on the one hand, from three? Now, there's no question that it is possible to separate three from one and two. It is possible. The question I'm putting to you is, is it desirable? Let me just give you an example from *USA Today* from five days ago. Probably many of you saw the article, which contains a good example. Plus, some of you are from Pennsylvania and are no doubt aware of this particular ministry. This short quote says that, "'Jesus wants people to have skills,' says Reverend Herbert Lusk, Pastor of the Greater Exodus Baptist Church in Philadelphia which offers a government-funded job training program through an affiliated non-profit corporation." And as part of the program, "trainees know they can drop in at a daily lunchtime Bible class with pastor Lusk in the adjacent church anytime they choose, or not."[1] Well that's compartmentalization. They run their jobs program. They even spatially separate the Bible study—they have the luxury of two buildings. And so the job training program takes place in one building, but everybody knows that for lunch hour, you can go to the Bible study next door, but you don't have to. Apparently many do, and certainly for Christians there is going to be spiritual nourishment and study, and for those who aren't Christians, it can't help but have a proselytizing or evangelism component to that Bible study. You can compartmentalize (I have yet to come up with a better word for *compartmentalize*), and our question here is (which was in fact raised this morning and not answered), Is it desirable?

Let me use Charitable Choice as a sort of baseline for all of us to shoot at. You can either say, yes, that strikes the right balance, or no, it went too far or didn't go far enough, but at least it's a baseline. And most all of us here know pretty much what Charitable Choice provides for. But, anytime I talk about Charitable Choice, I make three points. Many of you have heard these before, but I think it's critical that we keep repeating these points, almost like a credo that one says over and over again. When Charitable Choice was written, it had three principles in mind, and they're intertwined throughout the legislation. You are not going to understand it unless you get these three principles down.

I'll state them in no particular order. First, government is not to discriminate against a provider on the basis of religion. Second, a primary concern of Charitable Choice was to preserve the institutional integrity of a faith-based organization, notwithstanding that they elected to take governmental funding.

And, third, the legislation aims to protect the free exercise rights of the recipients of the welfare benefits. The third one hasn't been touched on, so far, at this conference. I mention this because E. J. Dionne mentioned free exercise, but he was talking about the providers. Here, under principle three, I'm talking about the free exercise of the people receiving benefits. They qualify for benefits, but we don't want to impinge upon their free exercise rights.

Let me just say something about nondiscrimination by government as to the first point. Charitable Choice does not mean that faith-based organizations will be

funded by government. It just means that they're put on a level playing field. It just means that they will no longer be discriminated against. But they still have to do the job. And if they can't do the job, or because somebody else can do the job better, they're not going to get the government contract, they're not going to be able to receive vouchers. I think there is a huge myth out there that Charitable Choice means faith-based organizations will get funding. This is simply false. Only if they can deliver better than their competitors will

Legal scholar Carl Esbeck discusses the recent tendency of the courts toward a "neutrality theory" interpretation of the First Amendment as the Interfaith Community Network's Rita Getman and The Bradley Foundation's Mike Hartmann listen.

they get funded. Charitable Choice just means they won't be discriminated against.

I had intended to elaborate only a little bit on how the autonomy of FBOs is protected. I now think, based on this morning, that a lot of our conversation here will be focused on how Charitable Choice tries to protect autonomy, maybe fails to do so, or does so in ways that do more harm than good. You'll have to make your own conclusions.

Let me just say a little about the larger issue concerning whether Charitable Choice violates the establishment clause. We don't know. I think not, at least given the general trajectory of the U.S. Supreme Court which is toward what I call "neutrality theory," what Steve Monsma calls "positive neutrality," what yet others call "equal treatment." Simply stated, neutrality theory says that if you're dealing with governmental benefits, the government treats all similarly situated groups the same in terms of eligibility. That's where the word *neutral* comes from: the same, without regarding religion. Program neutrality does not violate the establishment clause. There are really two requirements: that the government program has a secular purpose when dealing with the needy; and second, that all similarly situated groups be treated the same.

At that point, the establishment clause backs off and leads to private choice. Most concerns about government-religion relations are now heavily influenced by neutrality theory, at least since the late 1980s when neutrality began to emerge in court cases. It became a powerful presence in 1995 through the Supreme Court's Rosenberg case, then again in 1997 in the Agostini case, and now in *Mitchell vs. Helms*, which concerns a federal program that has neutrally funded K-12 schools since 1965. Mitchell involves the constitutionality of giving the same federal benefits to all schools, K-12, public or private, sectarian or non-sectarian, in distributing educational equipment. Back in 1965 it was overhead projectors, today of course, it's computers and all the appropriate software. Based on the oral arguments, we expect that this federal program which has been around for almost 35 years will be upheld. If so, the Mitchell case will just be one more installment in what I'm calling the general trajectory of the Court in embracing neutrality theory.

With that, let's come back to the institutional autonomy question that was hinted at this morning. One of the provisions of Charitable Choice is that there is a variety of prophylactic protections of providers and their autonomy. But, after the legislation was introduced, an amendment coming in through Packwood's staff, who was chair of the appropriate Senate committee, put in section 604a(j) called "limitations to use of funding for certain purposes." And the provision is really short: "No funds provided directly to institutions or organizations to provide services and administer programs under the foregoing sections shall be expended for sectarian worship, instruction, or prosyletization." If the funding is indirect through vouchers or certificates, this provision doesn't apply. Now this is because of a line of Supreme Court cases since 1970, holding that indirect funding was constitutional. But 604a(j) is applicable to direct funding. This brings us to two interrelated questions, which we will discuss. First, what does it mean? Second, is 604a(j) constitutionally required? What do you think?

Endnotes

1 Cathy Lynn Grossman, "Civic Service Based in Faith: There's Less Separating Church and the State of Social Action," *USA Today*, April 20, 2000.

What Public Officials Need to Know and Do about Charitable Choice

Bob Wineburg, among others, has reminded me several times about a haunting problem which is in fact one of my criticisms of the welfare law as well. The law assumed that we could go from essentially a government-run system of fiscal benefits to a system in which people receive community supports. But we all know that it takes a long time to build community supports. Yet the law just said to start the time clock ticking and start cutting people off welfare even though we haven't built that community support system. In fact, we can see on the ground in many places that it is a slow process to build such a system. If you want faith-based groups involved and say it's okay because of Charitable Choice, and four years later we are still debating what Charitable Choice means, then it's hard to get faith-based groups involved in the way that is supposed to be available.

So, there is this problem of constructing or reconstructing the social safety net, something different than what we had before. I think that one tendency is for government officials to say, since it's not going to just develop by itself, that we have to make it happen. So we should figure out what role the faith community will play and then give it its slot, so to speak. A number of states have said, "We know what the churches ought to do. They ought to do mentoring or they ought to provide community service positions, or they ought to do this or that," and the officials start to plan and design accordingly. The positive result is that there will be a network, but the negative thing is that the churches say, "Wait a second, you never talked to us first. You just told us what we were going to do. It's as if we are a different set of policy instruments that you're now going to pick up and use as you wish." It just doesn't work that way. It's a problem, both because the churches say, maybe that's not our role, that's not what we want to do, that's not what we're best at. That's a problem. And there is the problem that not all faith-based organizations are churches, and for the government to say the way the faith communities can get engaged in a new way is by working through congregations ignores a wide range of other kinds of faith-based organizations out there. I don't think this kind of government initiative works, and the reaction out there is very negative in the faith community.

Now, I think one of the beauties of Charitable Choice is that government doesn't have to make such plans. It doesn't have to figure out if faith-based organizations in general are more effective, which is quite impossible for us to answer. There are some very ineffective faith-based organizations. Officials don't have to figure out any of that. What they have to do is get rid of the barriers that made it impossible for faith-based organizations to compete. They should have protections in place for the recipients and for the religious character of the groups, and then let those organizations come forward and say what it is that they would like to contribute. That's what Charitable Choice is. It doesn't mark out a position for these groups, it just says they ought to have a chance.

Nevertheless, having said all that, it's not sufficient for government only to change its formal rules. To have a fruitful relationship between the government and these organizations takes more than Charitable Choice—because there need to be more things happening than Charitable Choice, and also because creating this new network requires more than just having some new rules. New initiatives are needed. So I want to talk a little bit about this more complex thing.

A key preliminary question to ask is, why collaborate with government? It's such a mess, so why bother doing it? I will then talk a little bit about barriers and some solutions to them, and then about Charitable Choice not being implemented.

I personally believe that the best society cannot be defined as the one with the most extensive and effective welfare state. The best thing is to have needs dealt with in other kinds of ways. So, personal responsibility, family support, mutual assistance, a civil society based upon people working out of their free will for the sake of each other—these are all the most critical means of caring for people's needs. I think, nevertheless, that the government may need to get involved. Let me quickly run through some reasons why that might be the case.

Helping You, Helping Me is the title of a book about energizing church-based volunteers. And one of the messages in that book, and one of the messages that is in all good teaching about volunteers, is that the volunteer ought to find what they're best at; otherwise they're going to burn out, they're not going to stick with it, it's not going to be their gift, and so on. That's a good message for the volunteer, but, of course, regardless of whether or not you can find a volunteer best suited to do something, some things just need to get done. So the volunteer impulse and the needs don't automatically fit together. Some jobs are popular, and some needs are not. But those needs have to be met somehow.

Individualized attention is one of the strengths of many community organizations and faith-based organizations. And yet there is the need for a certain level of standards to be met, because they're fellow citizens, because they're human and need to be looked after in some way, and not just to get any kind of individualized attention. It's wonderful to have an outpouring of generosity, but care needs to be there whether or not people feel particularly generous at a given time. Organizations ought to focus on their mission—otherwise, how can they persist, how can they do their best thing? But, beyond all the organizations focusing on their own missions, there has to be some way to be sure that society keeps its overall responsibility to make sure critical needs are not neglected. This public justice mission is important and is not the mission of any of these particular faith-based organizations. Asset development and empowerment are great ideas. Find out where a family's or neighborhood's strengths are and then build on

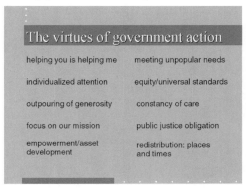

The virtues of government action

helping you is helping me	meeting unpopular needs
individualized attention	equity/universal standards
outpouring of generosity	constancy of care
focus on our mission	public justice obligation
empowerment/asset development	redistribution: places and times

them. But there are some issues about redistribution that still need to be taken into account: here is the poor community, and there are the places that have funding resources. A community may have plenty of resources at one time and not another.

I think that for reasons such as these, among others, it is important to have some kind of public justice or governmental function, some overarching perspective on things, and not just a view of society and needs from the underside and the volunteers of the faith-based organizations. So, I would suggest that collaboration between faith-based organizations and the government can be something that's important and necessary, depending on the nature of the need and the strengths and characteristics of government on the one side, and faith-based organizations on the other. But if that's the case, then the challenge is to devise kinds of collaboration that preserve the strengths and characteristics of government, but also of the faith-based organizations as well. So it's not either/or, government or charities; rather, they have to work together, and they have to work together in a fruitful kind of way.

I want to run quickly through some barriers and then spend a little bit of time on solutions. I'm looking at these from the viewpoint of faith-based organizations, and to some extent other nongovernmental organizations rather than from the government's side—which also has some legitimate concerns. It seems to me that if the government is seeking the collaboration of the faith-based organizations, that it needs to attend to the kinds of issues we will look at here.

Regarding Charitable Choice, one of the key barriers has been secularizing providers. Charitable Choice directly addresses these issues. It addresses the church/state dimension of financial relations. But that's only one of the dimensions of the relationship with government. And Charitable Choice by itself can't resolve all the other issues.

So what are some of these other issues? One of them is a *theological objection*. Some groups just do not want to work with government. That's their religious perspective, and that's the end of that story. Some groups have a *policy objection* to working with government: they don't like welfare reform, they don't like the way it's being carried out, they don't like the government in charge, they've got their axe to grind, whatever. That's what influences some faith-based organizations. We've discussed *secularization*. The idea that you *ought to serve everyone*, regardless of who they are, is something that some groups don't want to do. They think they can serve some groups better than other groups. *Dualism:* Carl Esbeck talked about it in the form of compartmentalization. Some groups don't want to have to divide religious and secular activities. There are issues of *dependency*, becoming too dependent on government or becoming too independent of your constituency. That's an issue for a lot of faith-based organizations when they think about working with the outside world. The *paperwork* worry: enough said. *Micro-management:* the government's going to tell you how to do things. *Fiscal accountability:* not just do you handle the money correctly, but can you document it and complete all the forms? And there's this whole issue of *capacity* that we haven't talked about. Sometimes when the government is looking to contract, it's looking for a thousand units of service, and a lot of groups don't want to do that. They're not geared up for that, they don't want to be that big. They want to help ten, fifteen, twenty families or something like that.

Charitable Choice and beyond

- a key barrier to fruitful collaboration has been past government rules that had a secularizing effect on fbos
- Charitable Choice addresses this barrier by requiring state and local governments to change the secularizing rules in their procurement programs

fbo issues	no funds	indirect support	funds
theological objection	•	•	
policy objection	•	•	•
secularization	•	•	•
must serve all	•	•	•
dualism	•	•	•
dependency/lose roots	•	•	•
paperwork	•	•	•
micromanagement	•	•	•
501(c)(3)	•	•	•
fiscal accountability	•	•	•
small capacity	•	•	•

If the relationship between the government and the organization doesn't involve any funding—referrals are a good example—I think all these things can be dealt with. It's a very loose relationship. In the case of indirect support—I'm thinking of things like tax credits or enhanced deductibility for contributions—then maybe a

501(c)(3) would be required in some cases (which can be a good step anyway), but otherwise all these concerns are met. Of course, no funding and indirect support make for a very loose relationship between government and these organizations. Sometimes you need a more steering relationship; there needs to be a more direct relationship. Government sometimes needs to purchase specific services, in which cases the relationship is tighter, and it becomes harder to deal with these concerns. But most of these things can be dealt with in one way or another, or the problems can be at least mitigated. Of course, a theological objection is different—if a group believes it is simply wrong to collaborate with government, then they need to stay true to that belief and maintain their distance.

So let's talk about a funding relationship. I think in the case of grants (and I'm thinking here of a grant to provide time-limited service) probably most of these concerns can be dealt with. Even the concern of having to serve everyone may be mitigated, if it's a designated grant in which you're going to serve this particular neighborhood, or some particular group. The paperwork can be minimized with a grant. It's a short-term type of thing, you report at the end on what you've done, and so on. Grants in general can be pretty flexible. If faith-based organizations don't want to deal with large amounts, just make the grants small and give lots of them. There are lots of ways to work around problems and help groups out.

Modes of Financial Relationship			
fbo issues	vouchers	grants	contracts
theological objection			
policy objection	•	•	
secularization	•	•	•
must serve all	•	•	•
dualism	•		
dependency/lose roots	•	•	•
paperwork	•	•	•
micromanagement	•	•	•
501(c)(3)	•	•	•
fiscal accountability	•	•	•
small capacity	•	•	•

I think vouchers also lend themselves well to dealing with these kinds of concerns. By definition, you're figuring there will be multiple providers. Vouchers give an indirect relationship with government, an arm's length relationship, so groups don't feel like they're committed to all that government policy, they are only providing a piece of the service. If the rules are appropriate, there's not a secularization threat; the groups are not serving everyone. Under Charitable Choice they don't have to extensively compartmentalize in the case of vouchers. So I think vouchers are a clean way to deal with most of the objections that faith-based organizations have.

Redesigned contracts can't solve all of these problems, but they can solve most of them. I left in dualism as an issue you can't avoid because Charitable Choice requires compartmentalization, period. And because contracting is a close connection with the government, if groups don't want to be identified by the government, then they ought not to get contracts. But I think for all of the rest of the concerns, when it is well-constructed, even contracting can be flexible.

If the objection is secularization, the solution is to comply fully with Charitable Choice. If the concern is that you've got to serve everyone, one way around that is to have multiple contracts or subcontracting, or to gather a number of groups as part of a consortium in which they agree who's going to take what part of the population. That's a way to structure things which may require government to help out. The government may have to say we're going to break down the amount of money so it's going to be required that a multiple number of groups get involved. It may require contractors to subcontract, or it might encourage a consortium, a neighborhood network that will work together to serve. So the government can facilitate getting around this barrier.

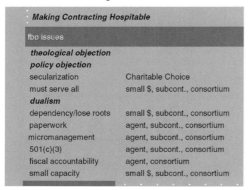

Making Contracting Hospitable	
fbo issues	
theological objection	
policy objection	
secularization	Charitable Choice
must serve all	small $, subcont., consortium
dualism	
dependency/lose roots	small $, subcont., consortium
paperwork	agent, subcont., consortium
micromanagement	agent, subcont., consortium
501(c)(3)	agent, subcont., consortium
fiscal accountability	agent, consortium
small capacity	small $, subcont., consortium

The same thing is true with the problem of dependency. Subcontracting makes government share the funds, which reduces dependency. Regarding the paperwork burden: subcontracting takes away some of that load, as does being part of a consortium or a network. Having a fiscal agent is what some churches are doing. They look to an established charity to be their agent, which takes away some of the paperwork burden. And government can either impede this or help it by the kinds of rules it creates. The same thing with micro-management, or the 501(c)(3) requirement—if the faith group can be a subcontractor, then it may be shielded from the pressure or requirements. Fiscal accountability can be dealt with by an agent. If the organization doesn't have a huge capacity, make the contracts very small, have liberal subcontracting possibilities or encourage a consortium to form.

Thus even under contracting, which is the most restrictive way of relating, with fruitful collaboration, government can open up opportunities for faith-based organizations, small groups, and groups that haven't done this kind of thing before.

What can government do to help build these constructive relationships? One thing it can do is choose the right kind of relationship. For example if it wants to work with a group such as Teen Challenge, it has to turn to vouchers or tax credits or something like that. If it wants to work with neighborhood groups, then it should think about subcontracting opportunities. Or maybe the grants can be kept really small, or vouchers can be used.

The procurement process has to be opened up. That's to say, instead of just sitting there and hoping people will come to you, go out into the community and let people know that there are opportunities.

Procurement itself needs to be reengineered. Requests for proposals (RFPs)should be slimmed down—forty pages instead of four hundred. Making contracts smaller so there are multiple contracts helps a lot. Judging by results instead of by process can reduce red tape. Requiring subcontracting or fiscal agents can help. Things like these are all ways of helping new players get into the game.

If programs are designed to be community-rooted, that opens up the opportunity for new kinds of groups to be involved. If you define your program as just the kind of thing you do nine to five in a classroom, then there is no reason for other groups to get involved, and they may not have any particular benefit to offer. Reaching out to the faith community and the community in general, offering technical assistance, and so on—these kinds of things are ways of linking to faith and community organizations.

However, in many cases if the secularizing rules are still there, then a lot of the groups just won't come to the table anyway. So, one of the issues is that if you go with Charitable Choice, you ought to reengineer, and if you reengineer, you ought to do Charitable Choice. They have to go together to really engage the faith-based organizations.

Almost four years after Charitable Choice was initially passed, only a few states have decisively embraced it. Arizona is one, Texas, Wisconsin, Ohio, and Indiana, are others. There are localities here and there that have said, "This is going to be the way we do things," but only a few states have fully committed themselves. Many states have just said, "What we're already doing is close enough; we don't have to change." Some states haven't been paying enough attention to this to even know about the new requirements. Some states are knowingly in violation.

Massachusetts is a state that just says, "We think that we're following the First Amendment, we don't care what Charitable Choice says." On top of that, they say that faith-based organizations could never come up to their exalted standards anyway, so why bother to work with them. I don't think that's quite what the law requires. They get a "U" for "unsatisfactory." Mississippi, started their Faith and Families program, which is good, but is not Charitable Choice; it recruited churches to provide volunteer services, but the State's procurement is what it's always been. The official there told me that he thought Charitable Choice was optional for states. Mississippi just didn't want to do it.

New York State is doing what it has always done, which is to contract in a somewhat secularizing way, with a few exceptions. The procurement rules say contractors cannot be pervasively sectarian. There's some nasty language in the rules and regulations. I've talked to a lot of county commissioners and people at the top of the bureaucracy who want to change that policy. But the impulse to change seems to get caught up in the state's church-state battles that have been going on for many years. However, I talked to federal welfare-to-work officials for the New York region who are trying to get the state officials to apply Charitable Choice—and the federal officials are part of an administration that has not been very warm toward Charitable Choice.

Some counties in California have done some things, but the State has not gone far enough. That's an "I" for "insufficient." But the legislature has told the welfare bureaucracy that it must crank out some Charitable Choice regulations in the very near future. Essentially, what California did was give all welfare to the counties and just forgot to tell them about Charitable Choice. And as a result, many counties don't know the requirements. Religious groups have gone to officials and said "What about Charitable Choice?" I've heard stories about officials turning on their computers and doing an Internet search to find out about the laws they were supposed to be following. California will get better because the legislature is now requiring a change.

Charitable Choice in 9 states	
Texas	S+
Wisconsin	S
Michigan	I
Virginia	I
California	I
Illinois	I
New York	U
Mississippi	U
Massachusetts	U

Virginia has talked a lot about working with faith-based groups, but has done very little. But they now have a task force which has said that it's time to get going on this and to run through all their rules and regulations to make sure they can follow Charitable Choice. The legislature has now said they're going to start doing something.

Michigan is a very open state in many ways, but when it comes to Charitable Choice they just are kind of lukewarm. There are some people there who are pressing for a clean adoption of Charitable Choice. Now, I don't want to say that in all of Michigan, Virginia, and California no good things are going on, but this is a question about whether the language and the spirit of Charitable Choice is being boldly adopted or not. I just think it's not happening yet in Michigan.

Wisconsin has taken some specific positive steps to put Charitable Choice into place. It's in the statute books, and the governor has enforced it as a condition for the new welfare contract. I give Texas an "S+" for its efforts. It goes much beyond the other states. Its compliance is systematic and thorough, and officials keep working to make sure the government agencies keep clearing away barriers.

Government can collaborate fruitfully with faith-based organizations. But to do so, it has to work creatively to help knock down barriers and to meet the real concerns the groups have.

Thank you.

What the Faith Community Needs to Know and Do about Charitable Choice

I'll start out with a structure in mind that has three basic questions. The first is, "What is currently happening on the ground in terms of government-faith collaboration?" We have talked about what things we need for the future, how we explain Charitable Choice, where we plan to be in four years' time, and what we'd like to see implemented during that time. But there is some activity out there now about which it is worth making some observations. The second question is a narrow, prescriptive inquiry. Given the little that's out there and its scale and diversity, what can be done to improve what is already going on? And here I'm going to be brief because Stanley's presentation did a great job of pointing to the concrete improvements that need to happen in the situation surrounding current partnerships. The third question, which I will spend a little more time on is: What steps need to be taken, particularly by the faith community, to generally improve the climate for hospitable and fruitful collaboration between government and the faith sector? So those are the three questions.

Let me say several things by way of answering the first question, "What is the actual situation on the ground right now, in terms of the scope of the faith community's contribution in the whole arena of social services?" This picks up nicely on what Scott [Jensen] was saying at the end of our last discussion. There's more going on than many people realize. We've had language about faith-based groups being "Points of Light" —and I actually like that language—but it kind of masks the reality, because it suggests that there's not really that much going on, that there's just a lot of nice little individual things going on. So the phrase doesn't do justice to just how large-scale the faith community's involvement is. Bob Wineburg and his colleague Ram Cnaan have done us a good service in trying to put some "hard numbers" on the scale of what the faith community is doing in social services. Some of the numbers I'm about to read come from the recent book (*The Newer Deal*) by Ram Cnaan. One-third of all daycare in the United States is housed in religious buildings. Ninety-two percent of congregations report that they operate at least one kind of social service or welfare program. These congregations also report spending about $4.4 billion dollars annually on human services. And that doesn't even count all the money that goes into faith-based adoption and healthcare services or to religiously affiliated hospitals.

In his book, Cnaan estimates that congregations alone contribute some $36 billion annually to various social services. That's an impressive number, and then on top of it you can add the contributions made by private, nonprofit, faith-based organizations (FBOs), or what we would call the "para-church" movement. And we know that many, many para-church organizations are out there. So congregations are giving $36 billion annually, and then you add on to that the millions upon millions of dollars of services provided by nonprofit FBOs. A 1985 study, just a little out of date, by the Council on Foundations, looked at these nonprofit FBOs and estimated they spend between $7.5 and $8 billion dollars annually on services to individuals and communities in need. So, yes there are wonderful "Points of Light," and we really need to celebrate that. Quite a bit is going on.

Also, we can look at the more recent development of new partnerships between government and the faith community ("new" defined as post-1996 welfare reform). In the research that I've done, I've identified new activities in at least 28 states (and probably there are more than I have been able to find). Let me give you just a quick laundry list of the kind of stuff that's going on. We've been talking at this conference mainly about Charitable Choice initiatives exclusively, which usually ends up focusing us on direct financial contracting. But, really, the nature of government-faith collaboration is a lot more diverse than just the narrow issue of direct financial contracts. There are a lot of different kinds of non-financial collaboration. Often this is really a win-win situation where you can get the best assets of the faith community, and the best assets of the government, working together.

Let me mention some different kinds of things that are going on. There's a program in California called ACT (All Congregations Together). They're in a nonfinancial collaboration with the local Department of Social Services (DSS) by which they basically just provide little "oases of comfort" in the middle of the welfare office and the lobby there. You're a mom, you come in there with your three kids, you have to go through this long line of people to navigate your way through the system, one kid is fighting with another kid, etc.—this is just not a very happy situation—and you're getting frazzled even before you go and talk to your caseworker. And here's a church volunteer sitting at the ACT Help Desk, to be with you there right in the office, and also to problem-solve with you about what is available in terms of community resources for those services that you need, that the government is not able to provide. All those "falling-through-the-cracks" type of issues. So this partnership doesn't have any money involved with it, and yet it's a very helpful service to people in need.

There's an interesting program in Illinois called Partners for Hope, which actually is an umbrella over a number of different kinds of initiatives. The most common activity going on under the Partners for Hope umbrella is that the government is providing very, very small grants to individual congregations—small meaning literally between $1,000 and $5,000. And the congregations agree to be a point of practical help and information to individuals that go through the Temporary Assistance for Needy Families (TANF) program, which are able to secure employment but face one or another kind of barriers to getting started on that new job. Maybe they need to purchase some kind of uniform. Maybe they have a daycare situation in place, but no "backup" daycare plan. The caseworker will suggest to this individual, who is moving from welfare to work, "Go down to the Partners for Hope church in your neighborhood, and you can talk to Miss Susie Smith about some of the specific things you need to get in the door at the new job you just secured." And the church has some financial resources provided by the government (to which they can, on their own initiative, add their own church resources) to help that particular individual get in the door on the new job. There are literally several hundred of these sites around the state.

Probably all of you have heard of the Ten Point Coalition, the very exciting ministry going on in Boston and some other cities where the clergy literally walk the streets of some of the more dangerous neighborhoods. They become involved in a strong working relationship with law enforcement, juvenile justice, etc. to provide at-risk youth with other options than gangs. Again, there's not a lot of money involved in this kind of partnership, but it's just a new type of working relationship between an arm of government and the community. In Boston, during one two-year period, there was not a single gun-related youth homicide, and all of the urban criminologist researchers realized that this was a radically unexpected thing. They said, "What the heck is going on in Boston that doesn't seem to be going on anywhere else?" Well, government and law enforcement agencies have been very quick to credit the activity of the church volunteers and the clergy through the Ten Point Coalition that are walking the streets for this dramatic achievement.

The Jobs Partnership ministry has already been mentioned today; it's a very interesting sort of three-legged stool—a collaboration between churches, the business community, and in some of their sites, government, to provide job training and job placement from a faith perspective to un- and underemployed individuals. The Jobs Partnership has received an enormous amount of attention, because their graduation rate is over 80 percent, and perhaps more important, their job retention rate is 90 percent or better. In other words, 90 percent of their graduates are on the job for at least a year or two years. This model is being replicated all around the country.

There are also a variety of faith-based childcare initiatives that are happening. Again, some of this may not involve any kind of direct financial contracting. Just to give you an example, there's a wonderfully creative program in Minneapolis called

KidsCare where the churches have a friendly relationship with an arm of the local county DSS. It encourages TANF recipients who wish to start their own businesses as home daycare providers. A DSS caseworker might put a TANF recipient into an accreditation/training program provided by government, and the woman will go through all that, and get all of her licensing and registration and her "stamp of approval." But what they were finding was that these women, when they decided to launch their new businesses, realized that, "I need high-chairs and I need fire extinguishers, and I've gone through this accreditation, but I don't know as much as I'd like to know about what preschool kids need in terms of enrichment activities." And so these new businesswomen are legally able to begin a new life for themselves, and the government's done its job by getting her to that point, but then they kind of drop her.

So there's this wonderful program where the churches are coming alongside these women once they're accredited, and each church provides not only some financial support to buy the physical equipment that's needed for the home daycare, but many churches then go beyond that financial scholarship to an ongoing relationship. You have a group of volunteers that come in every Wednesday to the women's home daycare business and give her a break for two hours by putting on a little program—making crafts or salt maps or whatever. Or a professional preschool teacher who is in the congregation, meets with the new in-home daycare provider to give her a lot of leftover curriculum from the preschool, and give her all kinds of ideas about the fun activities that she can do with the kids. This is all so that her home daycare is not just a babysitting service, but really kind of a mini-learning environment. This is just a wonderful program that's put a couple hundred women into these businesses, and on average they're providing ten daycare slots. So it's not only a new career for the women going from welfare to work, but it's a provision of ten quality daycare slots that are affordable and that are local to all the other people in her neighborhood, who are also going from welfare to work and need to find good daycare.

Then of course, you've probably read about the transportation issues related to welfare reform. There are rural areas that have church buses shipping people on the 40-mile commute into the larger city area. In my own state, there's an interesting system that's been set up in one of our more rural counties in which a group of churches was able to get some funding from the Department of Transportation (DOT). With that, they bought this thing called a "people mover" van (like you see at the airports). It's called the "Circuit Rider" because it was a bunch of Methodists and other Wesleyan churches that provided the service—very creative! The Circuit Rider van that was purchased with the DOT funds literally makes a circle through this three-county area. At different points, the Methodist churches pick up the three people from their local community, get them to that point on the Circuit Rider's circular path, and pick them up where they get dropped off to take them to their job, etc. The churches act as "spokes in the wheel" to connect people to the Rider's path—an interesting partnership to get people to work.

So there's just a wide variety of stuff that's going on. I was glad to read Elliott Wright's two-page report on faith-based workforce development activity, as that is one of the more common things churches are getting into. The mentoring of people going from welfare to work—that's going on in at least 21 states. And additional mentoring programs are under development in another twenty states. So in almost every state in the country, there are new faith-based, welfare-to-work mentoring programs.

Hopefully, this gives you a sketch of what's going on—it's considerable and it's diverse.

I wanted to mention now, more specifically and in greater detail, some findings from the nine states that Stanley Carlson-Thies and I had a chance to study through the Charitable Choice Tracking Project. As a recent *USA Today* article on the study mentioned, we discovered 125 new partnerships (i.e., post -1996) in the nine states. Eighty-four of those were financial partnerships, the rest were non-financial arrangements. The number of customers or welfare recipients being served through the financial partnerships, by my most conservative estimate, was about 3,000 people. Our study drew a few tentative conclusions. Dan Coats made the point that before we rush to expand the Charitable Choice language into lots of other federal funding streams, we need to have a handle on how well it's going right now. I don't think in any way that our study provides a definitive answer, but it at least provides the first good look at it. I would say the word on the street is: "So far, so good."

Out of all the different religious providers I spoke with, only a handful raised any really serious concerns or complaints about their relationship with their government partner. Usually, their complaints had to do with two things. One, there sure is an awful lot of paperwork and that's really a pain. Two, while generally there's a strong sense that church-state issues haven't been a problem (and these FBOs haven't felt "squelched" in their religious expression), nonetheless they hunger for more precise guidelines, for someone to really tell them what they can, and cannot, do. And then they'd report that when they'd go back and ask their government partner what they could do, that person would scratch his head and say, "I don't know what you can and can't do either—but we have a good relationship, so we just trust you and so it's going to be okay." The providers "on the street" are very conscientious, and they really want to know what they can and can't do, they don't want to be in violation as they walk that tightrope between Charitable Choice's front end (with its protection of the religious identity and expression of the FBO), and Charitable Choice's "back end" —section J prohibiting "sectarian worship, instruction, and proselytization."

The partnerships that do exist represent a number of different kinds of arrangements. There are the direct financial contracts; these are the ones that are most relevant to the Charitable Choice guidelines. But twenty of the 84 financial collaborations were set up as an indirect funding arrangement, which is where we get back to Bill Raymond's work and Barbara Earl's work in terms of the important role of "intermediary institutions." These intermediaries can serve as a fiscal agent to receive the government funds, pass them through, and sort of "subcontract" with an individual FBO or congregation(s). Almost without exception, the religiously based service providers that were in this kind of indirect funding arrangement were quite enthusiastic about it. They were glad that they didn't have a direct financial relationship with government. They felt that the reporting requirements that their fiscal agent made of them were less burdensome than they would have been from government, and they had this sense of being one more step removed from a direct interface with government. This made them feel much better about the whole church-state issue.

I think one of the agenda items for the future is to explore how we can do more of this kind of indirect contacting and begin to specify what it should look like, and how we can create or strengthen these intermediary organizations.

There's also some very interesting "gifts-in-kind" activity happening out there; again it's not really a case of direct cash contracting between government and the faith group. We have interesting situations wherein churches in a local area are letting the Department of Human Services (DHS) come in and have office space in the church, so that the people in their local neighborhood, who would otherwise have to ride four buses to get to the government's "one stop" center, can meet with DHS officials locally. Or, alternatively, the government says to a Bill Raymond [former exec. Director of Good Samaritan Ministries in Holland, MI] kind of person, who's out there with credibility in the faith community, "We'll provide you with office space at the DHS—a phone, a desk, a computer—and you work on mobilizing individual churches to get involved and get educated in working with us to help our clients." Then in addition to this "gifts-in-kind" collaboration, of course there are a variety of non-financial relationships like the ones that I mentioned earlier, where there exist Memorandums of Understanding under which the DHS makes referrals of clients to various faith-based programs such as job training and so on.

As Stanley's presentation made clear, the government is at varying levels of compliance with Charitable Choice, with some states doing a pretty good job, like Texas and Wisconsin, and other states not doing a good job. One of the most important things that came out of the Tracking Study was the fact that there are a lot of new players in this faith-government collaboration. Fifty-seven percent of the partnerships that we've found were examples of groups that had no previous relationship with government. I think that that is an encouraging finding as we talk about wanting the faith community to get more involved in these things. Another interesting thing that came up, which a number of people have been curious about, is the relationship of our study to the findings from a survey by Professor Mark Chaves—the National Congregations study—completed a couple of years ago. Chaves' study basically asked church leaders whether, hypothetically in the future, they would be interested in partnering with government. Were they aware of Charitable Choice activities, and would it be something they would take advantage of? His research suggested that evangelical congregations would be the least likely to get involved in this at all and that African-American congregations would be the most likely to take advantage of it.

The study we did puts a little bit more "grey" on that kind of black and white analysis. On the one hand, it certainly was clear that out of the congregations involved in our study, there were more African-American congregations. However, out of all of the financial collaborations, 45 of them were brand new organizations that had never had a financial contract with the government. And out of that 45, twenty of them were evangelical organizations. So this suggests that the evangelical community is not necessarily completely standing on the sidelines saying, "No, we are never going to be involved in any kind of relationship with government"—which, I think, is what a quick reading of the Mark Chaves study could lead some to erroneously assume.

The second question was, "Where are there some areas for improvement in these current partnerships?" and here we can be very quick, because I think Stanley has already told us what most of the actual items there are. Public officials need to modify their procurement procedures; in only a few instances are the government officials really being aggressive about beefing up their mailing lists so as to include all FBOs, rather than the "old boy network" of religiously affiliated nonprofits with a long history of government partnership. When government staffers just follow the old procedures, they leave out large numbers of faith-based groups who then don't even "get into the loop"—because they never receive information from government agencies sending out Requests for Proposals. So this really needs to change. In addition, the average amounts of the contracts and grant programs need to change. There needs to be a scaling down. These newer players from the faith community often don't have the administrative capacity to handle a $250 million contract. But they do have the administrative capacity to handle a $25,000 contract. There needs to be a greater push to smaller-sized granting and contracting.

During the study process, every time I found a new partnership, my goal was to interview the primary government contact involved with it, as well as the primary leader of the faith-based side. Time after time, I would interview the primary government person, and they would be very enthusiastic about this new partnership. They would tell me the genesis of how it got started. They would wax enthusiastic about what the faith-based provider was doing and how this was going so well. And then I'd begin to ask them very specific questions about the nature of their contract or their formal Memorandum of Understanding, and they would say, "Oh, well I don't do that part." Here you have this Charitable-Choice-aware government staffer, a sympathetic, welcoming government official like Phyllis Bennett, who represents the new idea of wanting to work for good partnerships and is really sincerely committed to that—yet, this isn't the individual that is actually structuring the relationship with the partnering FBO! That formal structuring is being done by Joe Blow over in the contracts office, who rarely knows anything about the new Charitable Choice guidelines. So when the Phyllis-type government person sends the word down to the contracts department that "we're going to have a new partnership with Reverend Johnson," Joe just pulls out the old, standard, boilerplate contract, says to Reverend Johnson, "You sign there and there and there," and the Phyllis-person doesn't even know what the Joe down in the contracts office did! So there's this funky bureaucratic lack of knowledge of what the right hand and the left hand are doing, and how can they talk together. So that needs to change.

Moreover, I think that there's an attitudinal element that needs to change in the faith community, in terms of the folks that are currently involved. I was simultaneously encouraged and frightened by a common phrase or response that I got from the person on the faith side when I began to probe. I'd say, "Okay, well now you have this new contract, this new relationship; talk to me about the whole church-state thing, what's going on? Do you feel squelched? What do you do—do you use the Bible in your programming?" And usually what they'd say is, "We feel comfortable," and it would boil down to, "Our government contact is just a great woman. 'Cathy' comes over here, we have lunch, she knows what we're doing, and we're all just straightforward. We have this 'gentleman's agreement' and things are just sailing along and we feel really good about that." On the one hand, that's very encouraging because we want to see strong relationships of mutual trust between the faith groups and public officials, if these relationships are going to work. On the other hand, as Steve Monsma has pointed out in his work, this is a very precarious footing. It could break down. Perhaps currently there's no church-state problems, because good old "Cathy" has this wonderful meeting every week with her friends at the FBO. But what happens when Cathy leaves and the next guy comes in who's not nearly as sympathetic to this whole issue of collaboration? Meanwhile, Joe Blow down in contracts has written the contract with no protections for the FBO in the actual contract. It's just going along nicely, because Cathy is such a nice person and is so enthusiastic about what those faith-based groups are doing. So, there needs to be a real attitude change in the faith community to say, "Cathy, I love you, and I'm glad we're going out for bagels every week, but you know what, I want something. Could you put some protections right into our formal contract, since you might get fired?"

I personally think, coming from the evangelical subculture, this is just part of the weakness in the evangelical community. We are very trusting and very relational. Remember the scandal a couple of years ago where there was a type of pyramid scheme in which major evangelical institutions lost millions of dollars? Well, it all came about because all those top-level people making these decisions had been out to dinner so many times with the guy running the thing. There was just this sense that "I'm talking to you about the Lord," and it's all about personal relationships and nothing about the hard institutional guarantees that need to be settled.

My last component to address today is a sort of "laundry list" of what steps need to be taken, not just with the existing partnerships, but to improve the collaboration environment more generally. I think this can go under different kinds of headings. One heading is the whole area of the faith community in taking the lead in defining what that balance beam looks like between Charitable Choice's "front end"

Hudson Institute senior fellow Amy Sherman discusses the recent growth of faith-based welfare-to-work mentoring programs across America. Pew Charitable Trust's Kimon Sargeant looks on.

and "back end." I hope that when we break into our work groups and we work a little bit on the draft Code of Conduct, we'll make further progress in this regard. Rather than letting everyone else define this balance beam for us, why don't we in the faith community take the initiative, and say this is how we're going to define the balance beam and what it looks like, and these are the principles of good practice that we are going to commit to?

The second heading is the whole issue of building capacity within the faith community, and I think that there are a variety of things we can be doing. There need to be intermediary organizations. There are some groups that are doing direct service who need to be convinced that actually a more strategic thing for them to do would be to not increase their direct service, but to take on this new role as an intermediary organization or a fiscal agent so that other people can begin to do direct service. There needs to be "big sistering" kinds of activity occurring so that, within particular kinds of social service, groups can network. If there's a mega-church down the street that's running a very fine program, and there's a smaller church somewhere that wants to do similar work, then there needs to be a mentoring relationship, church-to-church, FBO-to-FBO, for that kind of ministry. And this is the kind of thing that we need to get the philanthropic community involved in. Barbara Earls made a wonderful point earlier: what's "sexy" to funders is direct provision. And we've got to be able to change that mindset in the philanthropic community by the faith community coming out and saying, "Well that might be what's sexy, but if you really want to increase our capacity, and our effectiveness, and the scale of what we do, then it's big sistering, it's training, it's intermediary organizations, it's all that 'second layer' kind of thing."

I also think that the faith community has to have a political role, maybe not direct lobbying, but certainly trying to be excited about Charitable Choice (and perhaps its expansion) and about a variety of other kinds or ways of partnering: tax credits, vouchers, etc. We certainly don't want this whole debate about faith and government collaboration to be truncated down to the narrow issue of Charitable Choice, because it's much bigger than that. There are other kinds of funding mechanisms and other kinds of partnership mechanisms that are very important.

Also in terms of capacity, there is again a mindset change desperately needed within the faith community concerning tracking and evaluating its own work. Just like we need a new mindset about the personal relationships—"those are great but let's get the protections in writing"—we also need a mindset that direct ministry isn't only about being "out there on the streets, hanging with the brothers." That's clearly the most important thing the FBOs do. But if you never have somebody back in the office talking about how many brothers are you hanging out with and how long you've been hanging out with them, you're never going to be able to document what you're doing. So it's not only the academic community that needs to come up with creative and sensitive measures of evaluating success by FBOs. The faith community itself needs to have a better mindset that, yes, effective ministry out on the street is a priority, but the ministry at home, the non-sexy tasks of sitting at your desk and filling out the reports, is also very important. That is ministry as much as being out on the street is ministry, because what you're doing inside your office is having an effect on the quality of what you're doing outside of the office.

Finally, the faith community has to wrestle with some key questions. Are there creative ways that we can actually do performance-based contracting? What do we need to do to sit down with government and say, "We're not opposed to the general idea of being evaluated according to our performance, but we are a small organization and we've got to find some new and creative ways to work with these kinds of contracts?"

I think another question the faith community really needs to wrestle with is this whole issue of quantity versus quality. Over and over again we're saying, "Our strong suit is that we treat the whole person. Our strong suit is that we do relational ministry." Well, maybe that's our strong suit because we work with thirty families, and thus we're able to serve every individual as a whole person. That suggests that we might not be able on Wednesday to meet the needs of thirty families and on Thursday meet the needs of three thousand families. And so we really need to be realistic about how we can retain the depth and quality of our service, and not get caught up in the idea that we should expand from thirty to three thousand.

I think another crucial question for the faith community to wrestle with is the whole issue of the relationship between the FBO and the church. I think there needs to be a lot of dialogue within the faith community about how can the nonprofit para-churches can have a mentality of a really close relationship with individual congregations. The faith-based group might be doing great at moving people through job training, and other services, but for long-term sustainability, the individual needs to be enfolded into a loving and nurturing community. The para-church is not the church; the para-church is not the congregation. It's a wonderful place and it's full of people who are caring and loving, but if you want to have a fifteen-year relationship with a small community of people, you need to be embedded into a congregation. And I think that sometimes the church and the para-church haven't talked about how they need to really be actively engaged in partnering, so that graduates of the FBOs' programs are indeed folded into nurturing communities for the long haul.

The last thing I'll say is that from the congregation's side, I think that we also have to be so careful to constantly talk about the unique value of the faith community; not just that we're good service providers. There's a whole host of other things we do in terms of what we could call "religious capital." If we allow the whole debate to become very utilitarian ("Why is the faith sector so great? Well, it's so great because it delivers the goods, it delivers all these services"), then we lose the fact that it's in the congregations where we can encourage and develop responsible, charitable citizens. We can challenge the parishioner to give the tithe or more to charity rather than just 2.5 percent. It's in the context of the church that we can say to the Christian guy that's somewhere high up in a large, for-profit human services company: "I'm going to take you out to breakfast, brother, because I want to know why your company is making five million off of this contract to serve TANF recipients and then is just pocketing it and not pouring it back into services for the poor. Brother, you have a Christian responsibility that trumps and influences your responsibility on the job." So there's an important work of discipleship that happens in the religious community that is absolutely critical. And if we allow the conversation about the faith community to be only about what good service we provide, and we forget that the religious institutions are to be nurturing people of good character, people of understanding, responsible businesspeople, etc., then we are really going to lose out.

Faith-based Organizations and the Challenge of Civil Society

I was visiting recently with the president of one of the country's biggest philanthropies who, in addition to spending ten years running this philanthropy, had spent a lifetime as an engineer consulting the automobile industry in America on how to make the automobile as a mode of transportation safer, more crashworthy, and more crash resistant. He said that he and his engineering colleagues had to recently inform the automobile industry that all the engineering improvements we as humans could conceive to make cars more crash-resistant had pretty much been exhausted. If the automobile industry wanted to continue to improve safety, he said, it would have to shift modes entirely in the direction of crash prevention.

He went on to say that it was kind of difficult for an automobile engineer to conceive of the form of engineering required to change people's attitudes and behaviors, that is, to engineer a car in a way that would help people prevent their own accidents.

This change in automobile safety engineering provides an interesting metaphor when we consider the kind of transformation that we're experiencing at the philosophical level of American society—and indeed throughout the world at the dawning of this new century. We're moving beyond what I would describe as a long fixation with the technical, the rational, and the material to a far more organic view of how to organize society and how to produce well-being. We as social sector organizers and practitioners ought to be articulating a vision of well-being, of individual well-being, of communal well-being, of societal well-being. There is a universal law that serves as our guide (it is perhaps out of favor to think so, but it is true nonetheless). You can go anywhere in the world—the third-world or the first-world, the highest levels of society or the lowest, prisons or free society—and you can find universal agreement on what it is that constitutes a good person, a good citizen, a good family, a good neighborhood, a good society, and a good nation. All of us are participants in the social sector where this work is going to be done.

I'm not anti-government. I'm not anti-politics. I do think, however, that the twentieth century relied so heavily upon top-down formulas and top-down partisan politics and prescriptions to solve problems that are far deeper than these approaches could reach. We're now in the middle of the unfolding of a new emphasis on the social sector, the third leg of the stool. The twentieth century was very much fixed on a polarity between the state and the market. There's been real emphasis during the course of this conference on the fact that there are some things only the state sector can do and there are some things the market sector does very well. We see that. We've been living in prosperity. But those are two legs on a three-legged stool, and a three-legged stool can't stand up on two legs. The social sector is where the action is going to be.

During his talk, Dan Coats was referring to an essay of mine in which I addressed the state of this debate and what I think it means for social policy and for civil society in the years to come. In the essay I cited Dick Morris—a political consultant perhaps discredited but nevertheless very insightful—who said the Democrats have a lock on the public sector and the Republicans have a lock on the private sector, but neither has the social sector. Perhaps as an invitation to a partisan fight, he said that the party which seizes upon the social sector and mobilizes it will gain the allegiance of generations to come. Michael Novak at the American Enterprise Institute put it more subtly when he said, "Those who give life and breath and amplitude to the social sector will win the allegiance of the American people and will govern."

Why is that? I'm involved in a social sector initiative which Joe Liebermann is co-leading, and he has said that this business of reinventing civic America is classically American. We are tapping into something that's deeply American, and one need not be nationalistic or jingoistic or whatever else to say that if there's anything good about America, it is this tendency to recover that which is lost. As we close this conference today, I would go so far as to say that all of us see ourselves as part of a larger national or international movement. We haven't even talked about the international movement to empower nongovernment organizations in general—a growing phenomenon and a fascinating thing in which people around the world are learning what we're learning at home: you can't sit upon a stool that has two legs. You can't replace command-and-control socialist states with a market alone. You need the social sector.

What does the social sector do? People in the faith-based charity movement are part of the ferment created largely by Robert Putnam's work, which has elevated the idea that we need a stronger civic community to create the social capital that democratic citizens need. They need the capacity to be helpful, trustful, respectful. You can take that idea around the world. The whole world is in need of social capital. So long as you're involved in your projects, not only are you involved in the practical task of meeting the needs of the poor, but you're part of this reawakening in the social sector to the need for an increased capacity among individuals to function well together in a free society. Toqueville said Americans are forever forming associations of a thousand kinds, some large, some small, some serious, some futile, some moral, some religious, some strictly social—groups of a thousand different kinds with Americans from all walks of life. Furthermore, this was a distinctive, classical American characteristic dating back to the beginning. It was important, he said, not only because it accomplished numerous projects and tasks in communities, but because it produced a transformation in the individual, which in turn profited society. He said the mind is enlarged, the heart is engaged, by the reciprocal influence that people have on one another.

So the debate about civil society, of which the faith-based charity movement is a part, should not just be a debate about how much government support and funding is appropriate. I think that, too, misses the point. That's an important discussion to have, and I don't want to posit the social sector as something that ought to be wholly voluntary and without public sector support. But we ought to be raising up awareness regarding the tremendous contribution that the social sector has to make to American society, broadly speaking. Not just in the lives of individuals who are being transformed by faith-based charities, but in terms of the reinvigoration of our democratic experiment generally. I really believe that we are just beginning to imagine in our consciousness as a people, the power of the voluntary sector and voluntary associations in undertaking a whole host of tasks which, for any number of reasons, can't be performed predominantly by the government.

Conservatives tend to minimize the role of government in charity. They tend, one can argue at least, to overemphasize the role of the state in remoralization. I think we've got to realize the place of voluntary associations in bringing about remoralization—by which I mean basic ethics, an aptitude toward such things as marriage, and a commitment to live out some notion of moral responsibility called the golden rule. I could go on with dozens of examples. These objectives were largely met through voluntary associations throughout American history. So to the extent that some of us want to recover some semblance of social order and social morals, we should go out and create voluntary associations to serve that task as well.

In such an interconnected world today, I don't think anybody, even on the front lines of the war on poverty, even within the context of faith-based charities, can dismiss the socializing effects of popular mass culture. We run into it everywhere. So to the degree that we Americans can work within this Toquevillian vision to serve the poor, we can also bring about transformation within our communities—and organize ourselves in the process for renewal throughout all of American society. I think we're in for potentially a tremendous period of renewal. My book, *America's Promise*, looked very extensively at the divided opinion of Americans on the issues of moral values. There has been a very high increase—almost to a stratospheric level—in concern about moral values, but there's also a dramatic tapering off of interest in the political or governmental sector as solvers of the problem.

Civil society is a third way with regard to the state versus the market on a host of issues. It is also a third way in the state versus the purely voluntary charity movement. If it's a third way in these areas, civil society is probably the third way as well in this area of remoralization.

Finally, we are at the beginning of a massive, and unprecedented, transfer of wealth. The baby boom generation will start inheriting three to four trillion by the years 2010-2015, and when that is combined with the wealth that we'll have created, there will be ten or fifteen trillion dollars to direct, potentially, to new purposes. That's available to do what? We'll have more than is needed for investing in private yachts and for the enjoyment of retirement—although that's okay with me too. This money ought to be captured and directed toward social sector initiatives. We need to bring together our collective minds to create vehicles, mechanisms, tax credit systems, and any number of approaches that would be available to tap these resources and channel them into this process of social reforms that we're talking about.

I think we're living in exciting times. I for one have gained enormously from the wisdom and from the experience of everybody here over the last couple of days. I appreciate the opportunity from Curt Smith and the Hudson Institute to share these thoughts.

While the text from the speeches consumes the most space within these pages, the discussion at the conference was equally significant. It was vigorous, lively, productive—and difficult to capture in a way that does it justice. Not only did it take place in officially allotted times following the speeches, it continued over meals and in the hallways of Wingspread's lovely facilities and surroundings. Conference participants came from a variety of backgrounds and organizations. They held viewpoints on a range of issues that differed sharply from one another. And yet they displayed the highest regard for each other and were possessed of an admirable commitment to reaching consensus on the most important issues facing both government officials and faith community leaders.

Throughout the conference, five general topics were often and openly debated and discussed. These five were not proposed in advance but rather "emerged" in the dialogues following the speeches. Of course, more than these topics were discussed, but these five represent the most salient points. What follows has been improved by comments and suggestions from conference participants.

Evaluation, Research, and Monitoring Faith-Based Service Providers

After every speech, conference participants revisited the growing conviction among practitioners, public officials, policy makers, and academics that we suffer from a dearth of solid research on the effectiveness of faith-based programs. Much anecdotal evidence exists to support the belief that faith-based providers succeed where their secular counterparts fail, but we have very little actual evaluation and research to support, or counter, this claim. The group agreed that it is time to move beyond mere rhetorical support of these organizations to a well-grounded understanding of their particular strengths and weaknesses when compared to private and public providers offering the same kinds of services. Also, insofar as faith-based organizations are willing to partner with governmental agencies to provide services, participants strongly believed that they should be equally willing to be evaluated. Evaluation should be required of anyone entering into the public's trust to provide services either with tax dollars or in conjunction with agencies spending public money.

1. Monitoring and assessing the effectiveness of these programs should do two things: It should enable us to know what kinds of faith-based organizations produce what kinds of results, and under what conditions. Do organizations that are religiously demanding produce different results than those that are less so? What changes occur when we consider the level of bureaucracy possessed by each organization? Evaluation standards should be results-oriented in a way that applies across various kinds of providers. One good reason for a strong results focus is to determine the degree to which results are linked to the nature of the service provided. Large corporate service providers, we may discover, do not achieve the results that smaller, more nimble faith-based organizations achieve. But we will never know this if we only focus upon monitoring processes, which is too often the case, rather than upon commonly-shared criteria for real outcomes.

2. Evaluation and monitoring should also aim at helping faith-based organizations—and the partnerships of which they are a part—improve their performance. Monitoring and evaluation should not only happen as part of the government's overall responsibility to ensure public funds are being used well, as is the issue in point number 1 above, but the larger philanthropic community should also engage in the effort to produce a body of research and evaluation aimed at improving the capacity and results of these organizations.

New, Innovative Partnerships to Produce Maximum Impact and Effectiveness

There was a general agreement among the conference participants that improvement is needed within local and national networks providing services to the poor and other troubled populations. In the age of post-welfare reform, it is of the utmost importance to facilitate new forms of partnership and collaboration to deal with the challenges to service delivery, funding, and administration when multiple players—private and public—are involved. As states and localities were given greater latitude in designing their anti-poverty strategies through federal welfare reform, public sector responsibility for low-income populations began shift-

UNC-Greensboro's Bob Wineburg (right) discusses the need for strengthened community-based social services networks as Don Willett, of the Texas Governor's Office, listens.

ing away from direct provision toward the coordination of services. And the private sector has been increasingly given a greater share of service delivery responsibility as both for-profit and nonprofit organizations have begun partnering and contracting with public agencies. The increased participation of faith-based organizations in this collaborative environment only complicates matters more. With increasing recognition, even reliance, on the contributions of grass-roots community efforts (including faith-based organizations) to fight poverty, government has been adopting a more collaborative strategy to address social problems. The group was largely favorable to the potential this general change represents for improved service delivery, but it also recognized that many communities have not prepared themselves to manage their responsibilities *as* a community.

Several different models and ideas for enhanced collaboration were introduced and discussed. They include the following:

1. Nonprofit intermediary organizations should be contacted and supported within communities wherever they can assist in leveraging the strength of smaller faith-based organizations. Often, intermediaries have been successful in rallying together large numbers of churches and other faith-based organizations to provide services to at-risk populations. Government agencies can deal with the intermediary as a community-based partner and contractor to provide training for these smaller organizations and enlist their support, either as subcontractors or as non-financial partners, in helping individuals and families in need of work. Intermediaries possess the organizational capacity to handle administrative details that often present a stumbling block for small faith-based organizations. Most communities have candidates to fill this intermediary role. They simply need to put more energy, resources, and imagination into the project of working more closely with them.

2. Philanthropic organizations can play a larger role in helping faith-based organizations produce results in their effort to help low-income families in their communities. Philanthropy can also help provide an array of other services necessary for community-based efforts, from technological tools for coordinating activities to intensive training and development—or any other services that are needed but generally difficult to create resources for.

3. Corporations can play a larger role in partnering with faith-based organizations to serve both the general interests of the community and the corporation. Recruitment tracks can be built in conjunction with the faith community to address employers' needs to fill jobs, churches can provide mentor-based employment training and preparation in partnership with employers, and so on. The possibilities here are hardly realized, and there is really no good reason why they should not be pursued.

Clarity on Funding Issues

One of the biggest issues facing government partnerships with the faith community is how to provide resources to religious organizations that deliver services. As we have seen through Amy Sherman's and Stanley Carlson-Thies' research, a variety of new partnerships has been facilitated by the Charitable Choice clause, which specifies conditions under which religious organizations may receive public funding. Many are non-financial relationships, and it was the general tendency of the group to suggest that these kinds of partnerships be encouraged and explored wherever possible. It is simply easier, and lawsuits are not tempted, when no public funds go into the hands of faith-based organizations. But despite the difficulties with financial relationships, the group generally held that public funding should remain a viable option for religious organizations which have carefully weighed the risks.

What follows are several recommendations of the conference:

1. While the group was divided, and admittedly unsure in the final analysis, about the need for a religious organization to form a separate 501(c)(3) through which to run its government-funded programs, it did agree that it was an important option for faith-based groups to consider. What E. J. Dionne has referred to as "St. 501(c)(3)" may ultimately protect religious organizations from mixing their "sectarian" purposes with their social service activities. But establishing a separate organization is no panacea. Without care, this step might not go far enough, leaving beneficiaries subject to religious pressures they should not have to undergo. Or it might go too far, resulting in a total evacuation of religious values from the services, so that the program is no different than any other secular offering. Or, an us/them divide may begin between those in the founding organization and the newly created nonprofit. But this arrangement helps with financial accountability, which is fundamentally important, participants agreed, because surely—somewhere, sometime—a lawsuit will emerge when public funds are mismanaged by a religious organization. Ultimately, it was agreed that individual circumstances will govern the prudence of such an arrangement, but it ought to be given serious consideration by any faith-based organization thinking about receiving public funds.

2. The conditions governing direct funds to faith-based organizations in the law do not apply to vouchers. For this reason, vouchers are ideal so long as there is a real and demonstrable choice to be made by individuals using vouchers for services.

3. Public officials need to consider how to best monitor the requirement that direct government funds not be used to pay for inherently religious activities. Religious organizations have to be sure to account carefully for government funds and to be able to demonstrate that the funds have only been used for designated pur-

poses. Public officials and religious organization leaders should discuss together which activities may be paid for with government funds and how to ensure adequate accounting for those funds. And in order to do this, they need to join together to define which kinds of activities qualify as the "sectarian worship, instruction, and proselytization" prohibited by Charitable Choice (since Charitable Choice does not do this for us).

4. Ultimately, non-financial collaborations should be encouraged in a variety of forms. Aside from establishing a separate 501(c)(3), there are other options. Religious organizations may surround a secular nonprofit organization under contract with a public agency with support, mentors, and other services. Or, a publicly funded service provider may decentralize some of its work into the faith community (i.e., hold job training classes in a religious organization's facilities with the support of its staff), provided its use of funds for the program is clearly in keeping with the law.

Education of Public Officials and Faith Leaders

The conference participants agreed that a more aggressive approach to education in the terms and conditions of Charitable Choice and related matters is necessary. As Stanley Carlson-Thies' presentation demonstrated, there exists an insufficient level of awareness of the conditions of the law by state and local officials responsible for upholding them. There is, it was agreed, a general resistance among social workers, legal professionals, academics, and public officials to partnership with faith groups, which often fosters potentially illegal behavior. The Charitable Choice clause is best viewed as a kind of civil rights protection for faith-based organizations; that is, it opens up service provision opportunities to them that they cannot rightfully be denied. Insofar as public officials routinely exclude religious organizations from the bidding process, they act in violation of the law. Beyond understanding the terms of Charitable Choice, public officials are often unfamiliar with the local faith community, which inhibits their outreach ability.

Likewise, faith-based organizations stand in need of education in the terms of Charitable Choice and related matters. The First Amendment does not exempt them from being scrutinized for use of public funds, and whichever standards apply to other government contractors and partners apply equally to them. They also need to understand that Charitable Choice protects the rights of beneficiaries who may not discriminated against for any reason or forced to participate in religious activities. Many leaders in the faith community understand these conditions, and many do not. It was generally agreed upon at the conference that Texas has provided a good example in its requirement that each of its ten human services districts have a faith liaison whose job it is to coordinate all relevant public activity with the faith community. This requirement forces a certain healthy level of cooperation within the public agencies at the same time that it offers education and technical assistance to religious organizations.

The Active Role of the Faith Community in Shaping the Future of the Debate

At a higher, less technical level, conference participants expressed great hope and interest in the faith community as an active contributor to the debate on religion's role in the public square. Faith leaders should not adopt a "wait and see" attitude about how the future will play out in terms of religion's relationship to public life. Rather, they should embrace the current openness to matters of faith as an opportunity to help define what that relationship will look like five, ten, even fifty years from now. E. J. Dionne expressed optimism about the development of a new publicly valid moral vocabulary, Dan Coats voiced hope that the faith community could help revive and inspire tired public institutions, and Don Eberly spoke of a "remoralization" of those valuable forms of shared public life that have been weakened in recent decades. All of the conference attendees had a marked sensibility about the strength of community-based religious organizations. And they agreed that these organizations are not well-suited to merely "take orders" from policy makers. Rather, they possess wisdom about the best way for the world of government and the world of faith to work together in a common effort to renew the communities whose roads, infrastructure, institutions, and citizens they share. Not only should faith leaders actively stand up and offer their voices to the public debate, but public officials, policy makers, and other secular gatekeepers of public opinion should reach out to the faith community with an open ear.

CHAPTER NINE

From its inception, this conference was billed as future-oriented. Participants arrived with an understanding that their job was to look to tomorrow, the week after, and the decade ahead. At the conclusion of the conference, they divided into three groups to design two codes of conduct, one for public officials and another for faith community leaders, and an agenda for researchers and evaluators.

It was decided during the conference that the best way to enter the decade ahead is with well-prepared marching orders—and each of the three communities to whom these recommendations are targeted could stand to have better marching orders than they currently have. These recommendations, however, are not intended to be the final word. They are only intended to start a productive public conversation about the best way for each of these communities to approach the future of government partnerships with the faith community, and to build consensus in the process. It should be noted that the recommendations to religious organizations are written in the form of a declaration in order to encourage faith communities and associations to do likewise.

It is our hope that what follows will be read, considered, debated, and taken further by additional future forums on this topic. The greater consensus and common understanding we have about the relationship between religion and the public square, the better we will be at avoiding unnecessary future shipwrecks. One well-publicized abuse of the relationship could sink the whole ship and take down a lot of surrounding boats as well. And so long as government and the faith sector share communities, serve the same individuals, and treat similar problems, we need as many boats sailing as possible.

Code of Conduct for Public Officials

1. When reaching out to the faith community, officials should make a specific attempt to reach all of its parts, keeping in mind that different denominations and faith groups have different avenues of access and lines of communication.

2. Involve representatives from the faith community at the earliest stages of planning—plan *with* the faith community and not *for* the faith community.

3. Reform procurement policies and practices to embody the Charitable Choice guidelines in letter and spirit. Develop explicit guidelines concerning what faith-based organizations may and may not do in the area of religious practices and speech. Designate a staff member to monitor compliance with the guidelines by both government and faith-based organizations.

4. Re-engineer procurement procedures to be friendlier to faith-based and community-based organizations:

    a) use smaller grant/contract amounts

    b) take steps to ensure that contracts don't go only to the usual (traditional, largest) vendors

    c) provide technical assistance to newcomers (government can establish a nonprofit incubator, disseminate information about existing sources of technical assistance, provide small grants to enable groups to improve their ability to compete for funds, etc.)

    d) in addition to removing from procurement documents language that bars participation by faith-based groups, include language that specifically welcomes their participation

    e) make the RFP process simpler

    f) when contracts/grants are made smaller, lower qualification and operational requirements proportionately

    g) develop alternative criteria for assessing the competence of potential providers who have been successfully serving but do not have a conventional track record

    h) seek private (or public/private) funding support for novice organizations to give them a year to develop adequate systems and procedures for collaboration with government as well as a documented track record of service and effectiveness

    i) develop and disseminate a "how to get started" guide for nonprofits (how to incorporate, accounting requirements, RFP process, building capacity, etc.)

5. Designate faith-community liaisons to reach out to the faith communities, to be a point of contact within government, to monitor how hospitable government is to collaboration, and to troubleshoot/cut red tape:

    a) an office of faith-based action attached to the governor's office

    b) high officials in relevant departments (welfare, workforce, social services)

    c) officials in regional and/or local offices (this may be a newly designated task of an existing staffer)

d) remember that such persons/offices need to be "bilingual": know the language and mores of both government and the (diverse parts of the) faith community and be trusted by both sectors.

6. Evaluate policies and practices to ensure, at a minimum, that they do not harm existing faith-based organizations and collaborative efforts. Better, intentionally develop or redesign policies and practices to create in the jurisdiction a positive environment for the flourishing of faith-based organizations and collaborations. For example, encourage non-financial collaborations as well as financial collaborations; enact tax-credit and tax-deduction policies that provide greater resources to faith-based organizations; eliminate unnecessary credential, licensing, and accreditation requirements for organizations and service providers; adopt liability protections for good-willed service providers; encourage volunteerism, etc. Don't start a new government program to provide a service if a faith-based or other community-based provider already provides the service adequately or can be assisted to do so.

7. For fruitful financial collaborations with the various kinds of faith-based (and community-based) organizations, government should use a variety of collaboration measures in addition to conventional contracting, such as vouchers, contracts with intermediary organizations (which in turn engage several faith-based organizations), or innovation grants (let the organizations pitch their own idea of what the critical problems are and how they can best be solved), and subcontracting.

8. To maximize freedom for, and the creativity of, faith-based organizations and also more effective assistance for the needy, evaluations of service organizations should be based on performance rather than credentials or process measures.

9. To ensure continuity and coordination of services when delivery is being devolved to the nongovernmental and private sectors, government should take care to create or find mechanisms that encourage sharing of information about needs and available services. To ensure a balance between needs and available services, for instance, a voucherized delivery system may need to be paired with a management structure that tracks need trends and recruits new providers as necessary. More generally, a decentralized service delivery system needs some mechanism enabling information to be shared and services to be coordinated between various government programs, faith-based and community-based

organizations (whether they collaborate with government or not), the business sector, social clubs, and the like.

10. Remember that changing government practice involving relations with faith-based organizations requires much more than changing statutes. Regulations require continual attention. A concerted effort needs to be made to change the bureaucratic culture from indifference or hostility to nontraditional partners to hospitality. This needs to occur at all levels of government so that, for instance, efforts by state officials to permit a more hospitable regulatory climate for faith-based organizations are not thwarted by uncooperative local officials.

11. To emphasize the importance of, and to measure progress toward, increasingly positive relations between government and the faith-based providers, departments should be required to report periodically on the number and nature of their collaborations and the innovations they are making to foster better relations.

12. Executive leadership is vital to changing how government relates to the faith communities. Governors and departmental leaders can emphasize the importance of hospitable relations by taking high-profile actions such as appointing liaisons, initiating a task force on barriers facing faith-based organizations and ways to overcome them, issuing executive orders on expected new practices, and getting the legislature to adopt Charitable Choice into the state's own statutes. Executives also play a vital role by continually challenging those under them to demonstrably make progress toward improved relations.

13. Government should always remember that faith-based organizations, even if they are contractually delivering services, are never just service vendors. Fruitful relations are respectful ones in which government accepts the need of faith-based providers to advocate on behalf of clients as well as provide services to them, and to critique as well as collaborate with government.

14. Systematically work to clear away unnecessary and overly bureaucratic regulation of nongovernmental organizations and micromanaging procurement requirements. Such reforms will also create a more hospitable environment for faith-based organizations. At the same time, be mindful of any particular issues of special concern to the faith communities and ensure that those special problems also are resolved.

15. Because government is interested in preventing as well as responding to social problems, it should seek to encourage the moral mission (building character and virtues) of faith-based organizations and other institutions of civil society. For this reason, it should be as protective as possible of the ability of faith-based organizations to have a moralizing and transformative influence on those they serve and take care not to reduce such organizations to simple vendors of services that touch only body and brain, not soul and spirit.

16. While taking special and affirmative steps to make government hospitable to faith-based organizations, officials should take care not to adopt a quota mentality in which the organizations are inadvertently limited to only a certain percentage of contracts or only certain types of services (e.g., mentoring but not job training).

17. Given the distance that has developed between much of government and the faith community, it is important that government not only change its policies and practices to become hospitable to faith-based organizations but to actively market its new hospitality. Officials should find ways to send the message that a new day has dawned, that old practices are being changed, and that closed doors are now open. Officials can use examples of both bad relations and good collaborations to send a message about the need for and commitment to change.

18. To progress toward optimally fruitful collaborations, government officials should work both to lower as far as possible the requirements faith-based organizations must meet to be able to work with government (e.g., eliminating unnecessary certification requirements) and to raise the ability of faith-based organizations to meet the remaining requirements (e.g., by expanding the availability of technical assistance).

19. A critical role for a liaison official or office is to compile and maintain the most complete and accurate list possible of faith-based organizations that are potential collaborators with government or who provide services of interest to government. Such a list should be used to expand RFP mailing lists, for sending out information about government programs and rules of particular concern to the faith community, and for sending invitations to conferences and other events of special interest to faith-based organizations.

Code of Conduct for Religious Organizations

We members of the faith community, seeking to serve the needy, recognize the new opportunities to work in collaboration with government under the Charitable Choice section of the 1996 federal welfare reform act. We desire to be above reproach in all our dealings, including any potential collaborations with government. When we are recipients of public funding regulated by Charitable Choice, we therefore pledge to operate according to the following key principles:

1. **Compliance**: We agree to abide by the regulations of Charitable Choice. We openly affirm that government legitimately asserts certain requirements, and that, having agreed to accept the funds, we accept the duties attached (unless a gross injustice or issue of conscience would compel dissent). We commit to use only private funds, and never government contract funds, to underwrite inherently religious activities such as worship, sectarian instruction, and evangelism.

2. **Truthfulness and Transparency:** We commit ourselves to open, straightforward, clear, consistent communication about our religious identity to our volunteers, service beneficiaries, donors, and government. This means that our program descriptions will clearly depict our expectations of program participants, and explain which components of our programs are optional and which are mandatory. Our desire is to allow potential staff, volunteers, participants, and government contacts to make choices about involvement with our organization on the basis of full and accurate information about our program content, ethos, goals, and methodology

3. **Autonomy/Preservation of Religious Character:** We celebrate our identity as a faith-based organization and affirm Charitable Choice's guarantee to protect our religious character. We agree to refrain from using government funds to underwrite instruction that seeks to convert people to our religious faith—e.g., confessional activities such as study of sacred texts or classes in religious doctrine. But we maintain our right to identify our faith perspective in our educational endeavors (for example, inculcating morals consistent with the Bible).

4. **Witness:** We commit ourselves to a gentle and winsome public witness and to the creation of an environment in which staff, volunteers, and program participants are free to speak autobiographically about their own lives of faith. Our staff and volunteers are instructed to welcome and lovingly respond to spiritual inquiry and discussion initiated by program participants, while avoiding aggressive evangelism.

5. **Love of Neighbor:** We are committed to responding to our neighbors' diverse educational, vocational, financial, spiritual, emotional, and physical needs, treating each individual with dignity. We affirm "relational ministry" that helps the poor and needy connect to personal support networks—e.g., mentoring relationships with church members or support groups affiliated with the person's religious tradition—equipped to offer them emotional and practical help. Participation in such groups, however, will never be communicated as a prerequisite for receiving services. Our goal is to inform program participants of the options available to them for cultivating a personal network of support; they themselves must be free to determine whether or not to pursue those opportunities.

6. **Freedom from Religious Coercion:** We reject all forms of religious coercion and will not make the receipt of services contingent on the service beneficiary's participation in religious activities we sponsor. In programs underwritten with government funds, we pledge to refrain from making attendance in religious activities mandatory. We recognize that, for faith-based organizations operating rehabilitation programs in which participation in religious exercises is considered inherently vital to the participant's transformation (and in which participants freely agree to commit to the whole program), government contracts ought not to be sought, since these would require compartmentalizing program components. Rather, such programs should be funded fully by private means or by government vouchers.

7. **Nondiscrimination of Beneficiaries:** We will offer our services to all persons in need, regardless of their religious affiliation (or lack of affiliation).

8. **Mission Focus:** We agree to pursue financial collaboration with government only for those ventures that clearly fit within our sense of mission and calling, rather than adding on program elements simply because there is government money available to fund them. We pledge not to silence our prophetic voice. Hence, we will not hesitate to criticize government just because we have a contract with government.

9. **Evaluation:** We commit ourselves to credible and objective evaluation procedures and to maintaining clear and documented participant records so as to facilitate proper assessment of program performance.

10. **Golden Rule:** We commit ourselves to avoiding "turf-wars," gossip, and negative posturing in our competition with fellow faith-based organizations in bidding for government contracts; rather, we will treat our fellow religious and secular competitors as they themselves want to be treated.

11. **Financial Accountability:** We affirm that, as recipients of public funding, we are accountable to God, government, and to taxpayers. We will seek a standard of financial accountability and precision that is above reproach—including fully separate accounting of public and private dollars and transparency in all financial practices.

Agenda for Evaluators of Faith-based Service Providers
Beginning with the Right Assumptions

Research and evaluation of faith-based programs that assist individuals overcome barriers to gainful employment need to focus upon the most important variables and the right kinds of programs. Several assumptions are in order:

> *There is an insufficient body of literature documenting the effectiveness of faith-based social service providers, but the interest in having such a body of literature is widespread and growing.*

> *Not all faith-based organizations (FBOs) are effective, and not all secular programs are ineffective.*

> *Research should address not only whether or not programs are effective but should also shed light upon why they are or are not effective.*

> *Research should focus primarily upon programs that help individuals facing multiple barriers to employment, economic independence, and economic opportunity, because such research is at once very sparse and very important to the effort to reduce poverty.*

Measuring Effectiveness

As the second assumption suggests, effectiveness needs to be the goal of research and evaluation rather than a defense of the kind of organization providing the services. And effectiveness needs to be defined in terms that are commonly shared by the public and private communities.

Self-sufficient employment and family well-being should be the ultimate goals of a program, and all intermediate outcomes should be assessed in light of how well they serve these ends. To this end, family well-being, in particular, needs to be clearly defined, since its indicators are broader and less agreed-upon than those of economic independence.

Evaluators should make the measurement of outcomes their priority, not only an accounting of activities or simple cost-benefits; all activities and costs need to be assessed in terms of outcomes.

Intermediate outcomes (for example, obtaining a GED or a particular skills qualification, leaving a particular form of public assistance due to improved economic position, job retention and advancement beyond twelve months, and so on) need to be well-defined, accounted for, and comprehensively assessed.

The design of outcomes should be done collaboratively and with the participation of the population served, wherever possible.

Making Sound Cross-Sector Comparisons

In order to adequately assess the effectiveness of FBO service providers, comparisons among them and with secular service providers are needed. To fairly represent each group in comparisons, a typology of service providers is needed that would organize them according to:

One of four groups: highly religious FBOs (which can be further differentiated by the degree to which all or part of their activities have a strong religious character), religiously affiliated FBOs (which are officially religious but whose services are not religious in character), private secular organizations, and public agencies

Their level of bureaucratization: high, moderate, or low

Their level of resources: high ($500,000+), moderate ($100,000 - $500,000), low ($50,000 - $100,000), or very low (less than $50,000)

Their funding sources: percentage of public and private funds, and the kinds of public or private funds (i.e., which public agency's program, how much from individuals and foundations, etc.)

Accounting and Controlling for Extraneous Factors

The complexity of the barriers facing populations assisted by FBO service providers, together with the differences between communities in which they reside, presents a number of factors that must be considered by evaluators. These include, but are not limited to, the following, which must be thoroughly examined, altered, and added to:

Clients' self-selection of the programs that serve them

The severity of the barriers facing the clients, which presupposes an accurate indexing of barriers

The availability of employment, affordable housing, transportation, child care, and other community-based income supports

Implementing a Regional Evaluation Strategy

The assessment of individual programs is helpful in itself. However, evaluations that focus upon multiple service providers in the same geographic region provide a better understanding of program effectiveness. We recommend that evaluators design a research agenda for individual cities such as Philadelphia, which has a combination of active FBO service providers, competent researchers, and funders interested in the topic.

MARK ANDERSON
Representative, 29th District
State of Arizona

CHRIS BEEM
Program Officer, Democracy, Community
and Family
The Johnson Foundation

PHYLLIS IRENE BENNETT
Special Assistant,
Department of Public Welfare
Commonwealth of Pennsylvania

ALICIA CAMPBELL
Program Assistant
The Bradley Foundation

STANLEY CARLSON-THIES
Director of Social Policy Studies
Center for Public Justice

DAN COATS
Former U. S. Senator, Indiana
Special Counsel
Verner, Liipfert, Bernhard, McPherson &
Hand

E. J. DIONNE
Columnist
Washington Post
Senior Fellow
Governmental Studies Program of
The Brookings Institution

BARBARA EARLS
Director
Jubilee, North Carolina Council of Churches

DON EBERLY
Chairman & CEO
National Fatherhood Initiative
Director
Civil Society Project

CARL ESBECK
Director, Law Center
Christian Legal Society

RITA GETMAN
Executive Director
Interfaith Community Network

MICHAEL HARTMANN
Coordinator for Civic Renewal
The Bradley Foundation

JAY HEIN
Director, Welfare Policy Center
Hudson Institute

SCOTT JENSEN
Representative, 32nd District
Wisconsin State Assembly

DONNA LAWRENCE JONES
Pastor
Cookman United Methodist Church

Stephen Monsma
Professor and Chair
Social Science Division
Pepperdine University

Bobby Polito
President
Faith Works International

Bill Raymond
Faith Works Consulting Services

Kimon Sargeant
Program Officer, Religion Program
The Pew Charitable Trust

Amy Sherman
Senior Fellow, Welfare Policy Center
Hudson Institute
Urban Ministries Advisor
Trinity Presbyterian Church

Curt Smith
Chief Operating Officer
Hudson Institute

Ryan Streeter
Research Fellow, Welfare Policy Center
Hudson Institute

Heidi Rolland Unruh
Associate Director
Congregations and Communities Project,
Eastern Seminary
Policy Analyst
Evangelicals for Social Action

Don Willett
Research and Special Projects Director
Policy Division
Office of the Governor of Texas

Robert Wineburg
Professor, Department of Social Work
University of North Carolina at Greensboro

Karen Woods
State Faith-based Liaison
The Empowerment Network

Elliott Wright
Consultant
National Congress for Community Economic
Development

Dr. Stanley Carlson-Thies is Director of Social Policy at the Center for Public Justice and directs the Center's project to track the implementation and impact of Charitable Choice. He has written widely on the role of the faith community in welfare reform and the relationship between the public sector and religious organizations, and he has co-edited Welfare in America: Christian Perspectives on a Policy in Crisis *(Grand Rapids, MI: Eerdmans Publishing, 1996). Carlson-Thies frequently appears at conferences to address these and related issues.*

Dan Coats is a former United States Senator from Indiana. While in the Senate, Coats gained widespread attention when he pioneered the Project for American Renewal, which targeted increased participation of faith-based organizations in the public square. Senator Coats is currently Special Counsel at Verner, Liipfert, Bernhard, McPherson, and Hand, in Washington, D.C.

John J. DiIulio, Jr., is Frederic Fox Leadership Professor of Politics, Religion, and Civil Society at the University of Pennsylvania. He also heads up the new White House Office for Faith-Based and Community Initiatives, a position he has taken since writing the Preface for this volume. A senior fellow at the Manhattan Institute and the Brookings Institution, he directs Penn's Center for Research on Religion and Urban Civil Society. He also serves as senior counsel to Public/Private Ventures, which, with support from the Pew Charitable Trusts, is in the first year of an effort to see whether Philadelphia's faith-based organizations can partner with each other, with secular nonprofits, and with government agencies in developing effective citywide youth mentoring and after-school literacy programs.

E. J. Dionne, a Washington Post *columnist and Senior Fellow at the Brookings Institution, is a well-known commentator and frequent speaker on a range of issues related to civil society, democratic institutions, and American public life. Portions of this speech have appeared in the essay, "The Third Stage: New Frontiers of Religious Liberty," in* What's God Got to Do with the American Experiment *(Brookings Press, 2000), which Dionne and John DiIulio edited.*

Don Eberly is the Director of The Civil Society Project and Chairman and CEO of the National Fatherhood Initiative. Eberly is a noted public speaker, and he has written and edited a number of books on civil society. Most recently, he has edited The Civil Society Reader: The Classic Essays *(Rowman & Littlefield, 2000).*

Carl Esbeck is Director of the Center for Law and Religious Freedom, the advocacy division of the Christian Legal Society. He is presently on leave from the University of Missouri School of Law where he holds the Isabelle Wade & Paul C. Lyda Chair as Professor of Law. A well-known author and speaker on church and state issues, Esbeck was the progenitor of the Charitable Choice clause and is regularly involved in debates on religious liberty on Capitol Hill and across the country.

Dr. Amy Sherman is Senior Fellow at the Welfare Policy Center of Hudson Institute and Urban Ministries Advisor at Trinity Presbyterian Church in Charlottesville, VA. She is author of three books on the faith community's responsibility to the poor and community development. A frequent speaker at conferences, Dr. Sherman writes articles for a variety of publications and has authored the widely distributed Establishing a Church-based Welfare-to-Work Mentoring Ministry: A Practical "How-to" Guide *(Hudson Institute, 2000).*

Ryan Streeter is Research Fellow at Hudson Institute's Welfare Policy Center. He regularly writes, speaks, and advises on the civic importance of faith-based and community-based organizations. He treats these themes in his Transforming Charity: Toward a Results-Oriented Social Sector *(Indianapolis: Hudson Institute, 2001).*